If there was ever a book tailor-made to ⬛⬛⬛⬛⬛⬛⬛⬛ gle with control, this is it. I found myself ⬛⬛⬛⬛⬛⬛⬛⬛ en though I wouldn't have classified mysel⬛⬛⬛⬛⬛⬛⬛⬛ ve a lot to learn. Not only does Karen cha⬛⬛⬛⬛⬛⬛⬛⬛ he equips us to find the peace we crave as we ⬛⬛⬛ practically "let it go."

> —Lysa TerKeurst
> *New York Times* bestselling author of *Made to Crave* and
> *Unglued* and president of Proverbs 31 Ministries

Especially written for wives and mothers who try to control everyone and everything around them (believe me, I get this!), *Let. It. Go.* offers solid advice, wise counsel, and a healthy dose of humor. Full of why-to and how-to suggestions, plus helpful tools to measure what needs fixing, Karen Ehman's book goes right to the heart of the issue: "Are we trying to be godly, or are we trying to be God?"

> —Liz Curtis Higgs
> author of *The Girl's Still Got It*

Dear "I Am A Flagrant Control Freak" and "I Pretend Otherwise Or Know Someone Who Does,"

If you are ready or in the least bit curious about how to learn to truly get a grip on life, this is the book for you! Karen Ehman knows that in order to get that grip on life you so desire, you first have to let it go. Say what? Let it go? Trust me on this and continue reading. Let. It. Go. doesn't pull any punches (and I think we control-challenged women can and do appreciate such straightforwardness) as Karen melds her own often hilarious, sometimes painful, stories of learning how to quit calling all the shots with a lighthearted writing voice, sound biblical wisdom, and 'You can do this!' encouragement.

> —Julie Barnhill
> author of *She's Gonna Blow! Real Help for Mom's Dealing*
> *with Anger*, columnist for MOPS *MomSense*, and national
> and international keynote speaker

Let. It. Go. is a fresh, graceful way of pinning down what so often pins us down … control. Ehman masterfully tells her own story of breaking the control cyle in the life of her family. She teaches us to walk the line between control and trust, and to embrace the imperfect in our lives.

> —Gari Meacham
> author of *Spirit Hunger*

Let. It. Go. is a timely, inspiring, convicting, and freeing book that will take you back to the grace, acceptance, and peace God intended you to know. Karen has truly pinpointed and crafted a message that women are longing to hear—that God longs to lead us, bless us, hold us, and love us just as we are. Every woman I know needs to embrace the message Karen has so clearly communicated. Her vibrant stories, heart-felt insight, and practical spiritual applications will stay with you long after you have finished reading the book.

> —Sally Clarkson
> author of *Seasons of a Mother's Heart* and *The Mission*
> *of Motherhood*, cofounder of Whole Heart Ministries,
> and blogger at *I Take Joy* and *Mom Heart*

Packed with wisdom, wit, and wonderful tools to tame the control freak in all of us, *Let. It. Go.* is more than a book—it's a resource you'll want to keep for years! Karen doesn't just tell us what to do, she shows us what she's learned through her own struggles and helps us see how our need for control could be controlling us. Each chapter includes biblical teaching, everyday life examples, self-assessments, and practical tips that will give you the confidence you long for in your roles and relationships so that you can let go and lean more on the One who is ultimately in control!

> —Renee Swope
> bestselling author of *A Confident Heart*, radio cohost,
> and executive director of Proverbs 31 Ministries

Do you need biblical and practical wisdom for learning to walk by faith? This book is for you! Karen Ehman is funny, relatable, authentic, and inspiring. She speaks to the heart of every woman's built-in need to control, revealing what our true need really is—we need to "let it go."

> —Courtney Joseph
> blogger at Women Living Well Ministries

LET. IT. GO.

KAREN EHMAN

How to Stop Running the Show
and Start Walking in Faith

ZONDERVAN

LET. IT. GO.
Copyright © 2012 by Karen Ehman

Requests for information should be addressed to:
Zondervan, 3900 *Sparks Dr. SE, Grand Rapids, Michigan* 49546

ISBN 978-0-310-35740-7 (softcover)

ISBN 978-0-310-33394-4 (audio)

ISBN 978-0-310-33393-7 (ebook)

Library of Congress Cataloging-in-Publication Data

Ehman, Karen, 1964-
    Let, it, go : how to stop running the show and start walking in faith / By Karen Ehman.
      p. cm.
    Includes bibliographical references.
    ISBN 978-0-310-33392-0 (softcover)
    1. Christian women — Religious life. 2. Control (Psychology) — Religious aspects — Christianity. 3.
Submissiveness — Religious aspects — Christianity. I. Title.
    BV4527.E433 2012
    248.8'43 — dc23   2012015328

---

19 20 21 22 23 24 25 26 27 /LSC/ 26 25 24 23 22 21 20 19 18 17 16 15 14 13 12 11 10 9 8 7 6 5 4 3 2 1

To Mary Steinke

*My dear friend, accountability partner, personal prayer
warrior, and . . . okay . . . not gonna lie . . . occasional
cohort in crime.*

*You patiently love. You quietly serve. You fervently pray.
Your hidden work for the kingdom will be openly rewarded
in heaven one day. Then I'll be the one leaping to my feet,
clapping like crazy for my sweet, behind the scenes sister.*

*For your part in helping me become less of a control freak,
I humbly thank you. I can't imagine doing life without you
by my side and on your knees.*

Contents

Foreword

Growing up, I was a compliant child. When you're working in the entertainment industry, it's expected. You have to be disciplined and trained for the job; you have to take direction on the spot; and you have to keep up your grades, work late nights, and push through a work day even when you're sick. It wasn't easy, but I enjoyed it. What always made it worth it was hearing the words, "Good job! Well done, Candace" at the end of the day.

I learned early that if I followed instructions and focused on the constructive aspect of criticism, things went well for me. I had to get accustomed to allowing others to tell me what I was going to wear, how to style my hair, and how to apply my makeup. I grew used to others giving me notes and direction on how to improve my dialogue and scenes. This meant relinquishing control. In essence, that's what being an actor is really about—giving up one's natural tendencies to become someone else.

Isn't that what God does in each one of us when we surrender control and let him take the lead? Going against our own selfish desires, we allow God to shape us into the person *he* wants us to become.

I thought my daughter was going to be the same as me. I thought that she would have an adult perspective at a young age and that she would understand that complying and following direction can outweigh the struggle of trying to control everything yourself. But I'm afraid Natasha inherited the female "control gene."

Natasha has a desire to lead and control everything in her life (as many of us do). She's willing to sacrifice much in order to get her own way in spite of my rules. Most of the time, this results in consequences such as having her phone taken away, having time with friends limited, and missing out on some parties. While it's difficult to deal with at this stage of her life, I recognize the strong leadership skills she inherently has, and I long to see the day she uses that strength for the glory of God.

I'm helping Natasha shift her natural desire for control toward a supernatural reliance on the Lord. As a busy mom in charge of many aspects of my family's life, I am learning to do the same. After all, when I don't give up control, there are consequences for me too!

How do we fight the desire to micromanage and overcontrol? And in what ways can we encourage other women, including our daughters, to let go and trust God? How can we get-it-done, take-charge women learn to stop running the show and start walking in faith? These were just some of the questions Karen has answered in *Let. It. Go.* She gave me a fresh perspective on the issue of control, along with practical ideas for shepherding my daughter's heart.

Yes, it is part of our nature to want full control over our lives, but Karen's gentle whispers and witty nudges can help us learn to take our cues from the Great Director of life himself. Only then will we be able to fully surrender and with eager anticipation hear, "Good job. Well done!" from the Lord himself.

Come on now, gals. Let's play our part and LET. IT. GO.!

Candace Cameron Bure
Actress, producer, *New York Times*
bestselling author, and international speaker

PART 1

Why We Women Love to Run the Show

As far back as I can recall, I've liked to be in charge. As a girl I loved selecting a certain flavor of ice cream. As a teen I enjoyed choosing classes and pursuing particular activities. Now I love picking paint colors, selecting furniture—why, even custom-ordering a latte! Yes, exerting control and having a say is fun! It even imparts a sense of pride. Since being in charge seems to come naturally to women, isn't it a positive attribute? Or, carried to an extreme, can it instead cause conflict and heartache? Just why do we women love to run the show?

CHAPTER 1

Wired to Control

Control is a hard-edged word; it has — at least it seems to have — no poetry in it.
Judith Viorst

It is better to take refuge in the LORD than to trust in humans.
Psalm 118:8

I glanced once again at the oak mantel clock perched in my living room, hopeful that time had kindly ticked off another sixty minutes. I was anxious for the hours to accumulate, turning into days that would then form weeks. I strained my foggy mind trying to calculate. I hoped that when three or four more weeks passed, I might actually start to feel alive again.

But alas, the chiming heirloom piece was not my time-accruing friend that afternoon. In fact, only eleven meager minutes had elapsed since I'd last peered expectantly at its Roman- numeral-clad face.

It was the early fall of 1997, and I was pregnant with my third child. I had been diagnosed a repeat victim of what my doctor referred to as "severe hyperemesis."

Hyperemesis? That's a fancy medical expression that translates into layperson's terms as "morning sickness that lasts all day long." It was my new, intellectually impressive but least-favorite word. This hurricane of hyperemesis was chronic, constant, and downright debilitating. I'd never felt so sick in all my life.

With my first child, this condition lasted eight months. With baby number two it was seven. This time, however, I hoped the intense nausea would subside by month six, if it stayed true to its gone-a-month-earlier-each-time pattern.

No tricks or home remedies worked. Eating crackers before attempting to get out of bed each day only made me get sick even faster than when I arose with an empty stomach. Ingesting ground ginger didn't help. Or chewing fresh mint. Or downing any other herb or pill well-meaning friends sent my way.

I couldn't keep solid food down morning, noon, or even night, for that matter. Only sips of diluted chicken broth and occasional swigs of colored sports drinks would stay down. Usually. I had to resort to protein drinks and IVs during a few stints in the hospital to try to help me get well.

So I faced life in a tenuous state, feeling I had an awful case of the stomach flu coupled with the sensation of having just stepped off an upside-down, convoluting roller coaster directly onto a ship sailing off on the choppy high seas.

Okay. Maybe I exaggerate a tad. But the truth is this: there was only one thing worse than my ruthless, all-day queasiness. It was a frightening and foreign sensation that left my stomach untouched but invaded my thoughts and emotions every day. The feeling was that of being utterly out of control.

No Longer in Command

Now I wasn't out of control in the sense that I'd completely lost my senses. You know, the "she is completely out of control" way of describing someone who's behaving in an irrational manner. There was no need to call in the psychologist-turned-daytime-host of the latest self-help cable-television show. That wasn't the out-of-control state in which I found my little under-the-weather self.

Rather, I was squarely situated in a different out-of-control state—I was no longer able to be in command.

Of my home.

Of my children.

Of my schedule.

Of my appearance.

Of so many other basic elements over which we women are used to having jurisdiction.

I couldn't ensure that my kids were dressed in matching clothes (or that they were even dressed at all!). I was too infirm to insist they brush their teeth *all* the way to the back just like the dentist had instructed or to oversee them putting their toys away before bedtime. I couldn't pay the bills on time. Or return phone calls promptly. Or carry out any other task that might require me to actually sit up and think straight.

There were bright spots during my dark days, although I failed to see them at the time. So many people in our circle of life stepped up to serve. My family dined for months on meals that loving church members brought in, and dear friends took turns watching our kids (and their ailing mom) each day while my husband, Todd, went off to work.

Looking back, I see how God took care of every last detail, and I readily admit that neither my family nor my home suffered lasting consequences because of this season of sickness.

Instead, it was I who suffered—shaken to the core of who I thought I was. It was foreign soil to me, dwelling temporarily in out-of-control land. And honestly, it was a place I'm not sure I'd ever visited until my pregnancies forced me to dwell there.

Mission Control

Many women crave control. Why, we might even appear to emerge from the womb crouched and ready to manage, plan,

13

arrange, position, and take charge. We like to craft scenarios and situate people. Even young toddler girls can be observed lining their frilly dolls up or stacking toy dishes or bright building blocks in a way that suits their fancy. And heaven forbid that anyone should interfere with a girl's plan! These miniversions of us women often instinctively order and organize anything within their reach—objects, circumstances, and later on in life, even living, breathing human beings.

Young females not only desire to control their surroundings; they're actually pretty proficient at it. As an elementary student I noticed that the girls on my block liked coming up with the games our neighborhood gang would play. At school we loved to be selected for special duties, such as delivering papers to the principal's office. As we grew older, my girlfriends and I liked to organize, arrange, and get others fired up about planning a banquet or putting on a play. Being in charge energized us.

In defense of my gender, this is often a much-needed skill. A competent woman can run a bang-up PTA bake sale or plan a fabulous family reunion. She can juggle home, school, professional life, and church duties with downright riveting results! Being able to multitask, to craft duties and delegate tasks, is beneficial on many fronts. The problem lies with our failure to know where to draw the line, to differentiate between leading and bossing, to know the difference between simply taking charge and ultimately taking over.

Competency is a sought-after strength. But if carried to an extreme and left unchecked, our strengths can often morph into wretched weaknesses. We may carry these strengths of managing and positioning to such excess that they hinder our relationships both inside and outside the home. And our controlling nature often gives us fits when circumstances don't go as we'd planned.

We fret and worry and waste unnecessary time trying to remedy situations in which we have no business and where our perfectly powdered noses don't belong. Still we fuss and fume and stridently complain; we bark out orders (or subtly pout, depending on our personalities) and grow ourselves not-so-little ulcers over sometimes-diminutive things.

Scads of women carry this attribute of control into adulthood; some carry it into marriage and eventually into mothering, should kiddos come along. It seems to flow naturally. We transition seamlessly. And actually, this mode of operation is of great benefit to our gender. After all, with all that women must juggle in today's world, a little in-charge approach can only help, right?

Think about it. While there are numerous dads who invest time and effort in raising, caring for, and carting around their children, and who certainly shoulder their fair share of the load around the family's physical domain, more often than not, these duties fall on the maternal side of the job ledger.

As I sit at my writing desk now and glance over my day planner at the week marked out ahead, my eyes land on a list of duties I must perform for my family in the next seven days:

- Sign one child up at the district superintendent's office for middle school.

- Order science and English curriculum for another child whom I homeschool.

- Plan the week's menu.

- Grocery shop, as well as stop at the drugstore for prescriptions and at the department store for tennis-shoe laces.

- Prepare the meals and snacks for the week. (Okay, and

perhaps order a take-out pizza or two on the crazy-busy nights.)

- Make appointments for both boys at the eye doctor.
- Do a few loads of laundry (my kids do their own).
- Clean the house (supervising one child and delegating tasks to another).
- Reorganize the coat closets, getting them ready them for fall.
- Haul one child back and forth to football practice four nights of the week.
- Call three colleges to arrange visits for my high school son.
- Place a few online orders.
- Deposit money in the bank account from the family garage sale.
- Break down and clean up after the family garage sale, donating leftover items to charity.
- Call to check on three different aging parents, two of whom may be facing surgery.
- Mail a care package to my daughter, who lives in North Carolina.

Whew! I'm tired just typing out that list on my keyboard!

So while women may tend to be take-charge sorts, in our defense we often have a lot on our plates. Some gals possess a stack of plates that are almost ready to topple, the plates are laden so high. When we ladies are responsible for so many people and tasks, it seems natural, and even necessary, to call all the shots.

In fact, we can even attempt to glaze this grab for power with an opaque film of righteousness. After all, maybe we're taking God's directions to us in Colossians 3:23 seriously: "Work willingly at whatever you do, as though you were working for the Lord rather than for people" (NLT). Well, then, aren't we just being good church girls, trying to serve Jesus by being in charge of it all? Yep, that's it. We're simply being careful and conscientious.

Therein, fellow control freak of mine, lies the problem. There exists a minuscule line between being conscientious and being controlling. A marker so fine, we women cross it without even noticing that it's stretched out right there in front of us, waiting to trip us up. What we must do is determine the difference between being conscientious (our part) and being in control (God's job).

Two Stunning Revelations

That crisp Michigan autumn when I was barely able to be in charge of anything found me bordering on depression. I couldn't care for my two kids, cook a minimal meal, run the washer or dryer—not to mention sort the lights, whites, and darks—or carry out any of the other mostly mundane tasks of motherhood.

I recall lying on the sofa, hot tears soaking into a scratchy throw pillow, as two teens from our youth group came over to clean my house from filthy top to grimy bottom. My husband was a youth pastor, and many of the teenagers wanted to help our family out. I wish I could say I graciously accepted the domestic assistance the sweet girls willingly offered. Sadly, I did not. While I said nothing to them but to squeak out a weak "Thank you," inside I was a knotted, emotionally stressed mess.

I fretted over the dirty floors. I was embarrassed by the sticky soda spills that now acted as a messy magnet for lint and dirt. I was horror-struck that someone else had to deal with my grunge because I was too sick to sit up without fainting, let alone to wield a mop or whisk a broom.

The salty tears stung my face, making me feel more ill than I already was. My only escape was sleep. So I drifted off. As I did I prayed that when I awoke I'd miraculously feel better. Then I could get out of this miserable state and back into the driver's seat again.

I've had over a decade now to analyze what it was that bothered me so when I had to loosen my death grip on life's steering wheel. Was it a feeling of helplessness? Or was I concerned about my reputation, afraid of being labeled incapable on the home front, a place where I thought I had it all together?

Maybe I resented being viewed as lazy. Some women in my life were certain I couldn't be *that* sick, since they had breezed through their pregnancies with nary a trace of morning sickness.

Was it concern for my children, whom God had entrusted to me? Was I worried they wouldn't be cared for properly or that they would be emotionally damaged because they had an unwell mommy who was out of commission for long stretches of their toddler years?

Or was it old-fashioned guilt? Seeing my sweet husband be both mom and dad, as well as chief cook, sock sorter, and chauffer, made me feel to blame for his increased workload around the house. After all, he was already working more than forty-five hours a week at his marketplace job.

I think all those scenarios came somewhat into play. However, if I'm introspective and honest enough, I know deep down what bothered me most. It all centered on two new revelations I discovered back then that smacked me in the face for the very first time (but most definitely not for the last).

First, I did not fancy the fresh discovery that I was dispensable. Often, in my reasoning, I'd spun a saga to myself where I headlined as the "martyr mom" heroine. "You know," I'd declare, "things around here would totally fall apart without me. How would these people ever function if I weren't here? I am the glue that holds this family together."

Wrong! Lying there watching my family fare pretty well with me out of the picture was truly humbling. I thought they'd surely perish without martyr mom on the scene. On the contrary, they were doing just fine, thank you very much. For the first time as a parent, I had an inkling that maybe I really wasn't "all that and a whole-wheat baguette" as I'd imagined. (I know, I know. The phrase is "all that and a bag of chips," but I never get chips as the side at Panera Bread. I always get the whole-wheat baguette!)

While priding myself on being able to care for the children, run a home smoothly, and do it all with a big public smile, I was also building a little temple to my own perceived abilities. Yes, others could periodically perform domestic functions at my house or even care for my kids when Todd and I went on a date, but completely replace me? Never! I, my mind concluded, am simply irreplaceable.

Or so I'd thought.

Second, and what in all probability was at the crux of my crisis, was this stunning discovery: when I was unable to function, I was also unable to get my own way. (Cue the Frank Sinatra music, please.)

Much to my husband's shock, I was just too sick to voice an

opinion. Before, I had distinct views about everything from peanut butter to politics. The baby must be diapered a certain way, the fridge stocked in the manner I deemed most logical. I knew which dress Mackenzie looked best in for the Christmas pageant at church and which one made her look washed-out on stage.

I asserted my views openly and persuasively, and it usually translated into me getting my way. You know that old adage: "If Momma ain't happy, ain't nobody happy. If Papa ain't happy, who cares?" How true that rang at my house. Sadly, I made sure everyone shared in the misery if this momma wasn't happy. And being happy, I thought, meant getting my own way.

The Many Faces of Control

Why are women compelled to control? The answer is simple: because we have a false notion that it actually works. And when it appears that it isn't working, we think the remedy is found by exerting even greater control. Never in a million years would it cross our conniving minds that the answer in fact lies in letting go, not in tightening our grip. We'll explore this seemingly backward truth later.

What does control look like? No cookie cutters here. If you observe closely, you'll realize that not every woman controls in the same way. If you think only the loud, boisterous, and dominant sisters are the ones who struggle with this issue, you're misguided. We'll look more closely at the creative ways we try to control, but for the moment, consider how control dons many clever disguises. Here are just a few of them . . .

First, there is the soft-spoken saint, a sweet, helpful woman who says yes to every request whether it inconveniences her or not. You can count on her to come through in the clutch, and do so with a charming disposition. This woman controls by getting along selflessly. She is so agreeable that when it's her turn to ask for something, others will give in. After all, she is always so nice. She controls by her kindness. Although at times it may be genuine, at other times it's not. It's her means of getting her own meek and mousy way.

Then there is the enabler. If her child forgets his homework or lunch pail, she treks off across town to promptly deliver it. If her husband is a harsh man, always hurling hurtful words at her and others, she overlooks the insults directed at her and either runs interference or does damage control when his actions affect others. She crafts excuses for her loved ones' bad behavior, often absorbing the blame herself, even when it was clearly their fault. This woman controls by covering up. She wants her family to have a good reputation, so she seeks to build one all by herself, despite the lack of cooperation from her kin.

Next we have the victim or martyr. She controls not by yelling or barking out orders but by well-timed pouting and the occasional sigh. If a decision is made or a scenario is played out that she doesn't particularly care for, expect sorrow to appear on her face and dejection to come forth in her actions. Since others don't want to hurt her feelings or add to her sadness, they give in to her wishes instead. She gets her way not by stomping her feet but by dropping her smile. When approached, she most likely will say, "No, I'm fine. Don't worry about me. You just do what you want. I'll be okay." Her pouting is powerful. And it is also a creative form of control.

How about the people pleaser? She showers others with compliments. Lavishes coworkers with gifts. She says what you want to hear and makes it her goal to never ruffle any feathers. Ever the chameleon, she licks her finger and sticks it in the air to see which way the wind is blowing before jumping on the band-wagon. She may even change her opinion depending on whom she is with and what she estimates they'll want to hear. Her line of thinking is this: if everyone mentally elects her "Miss Congeniality" of the social circle, surely this will aid in her getting her way. After all, she'll be owed so many unspoken favors by so many people that they will happily give in to her wishes. This sister controls with feigned friendship.

Wired to Control

While our personalities and methods may vary, our goal is often the same. And I'd wager that at the root of our problem are exactly the same two issues I unearthed while confined to my sofa of sickness:

1. We want to feel indispensable.

2. We want to get our own way.

Although these two threads are common to the quests for control, an even stronger similar strand is often woven deep into our "I'll do it my way" souls.

We don't really trust God.

Oh, we believe *in* God. We know all about his wonderful characteristics and mighty acts. We know he is patient, loving, forgiving, powerful, ever near, always faithful. Why, he is perfect!

We may even read on the pages of our Bibles about men and women who trusted him with amazing results. But we doubt he'll really repeat this in our suburban, modern, everyday lives. We intellectually believe he does what is best for the world in general, but practically we behave as if in our individual situations, *we* still know what's best.

Our lips may say we trust him, but our actions say the opposite. "If it is to be, it is up to me" becomes our self-serving mantra. Deep in our hearts, however, we long for more.

Controlling is tiring. So is keeping up a good front. But how in the world will we ever change our well-worn patterns? They now feel so familiar, and to the familiar we are strangely drawn, even if we know the results are sometimes disastrous.

I think it starts with admitting that however it may manifest itself in our own unique personalities, we have a problem: our wiring is screwed up. Because of sin, we're wired to control everything ourselves. And it will take a Great Electrician to sort through our tangled mess of selfish motives and actions and attitudes and transform them into one smooth, humming connection to our Father.

Take it from a self-confessed control freak. It has been my experience, through the school of hard knocks, that there is vast freedom in pursuing a life lived *out* of our own control. So be encouraged. Once we recognize we have a problem, we can begin to seek and apply a righteous remedy, one not found in the pages of a self-help manual or on the screen of the latest psychologist's talk show, but one straight from the pages of Scripture.

Yes, the cure for our malady lies not in a pill or an old folklore remedy but in learning to walk lockstep with the Savior down the path of *his* choosing. We must be trained to embrace this dichotomy of a truth: in order to get a grip, we have to let go.

So sit tight, sister. Together we'll learn to discern a crucial life skill: how to control what we should and trust God with what we can't.

But first, let's take a little quiz to test our personal control quotient. (We'll be using such self-evaluation tools throughout our journey together.)

Finding Your Control Quotient

Answer the following questions on a scale of 1–5, using this key:

1. never
2. seldom
3. sometimes
4. usually
5. always

When it comes to making common, everyday decisions as part of a group, like which restaurant to eat at or what color to paint the office, I like to voice my opinion to ensure the outcome I desire.

    1   2   3   4   5

I would honestly say that in my personal relationships, I try to get people to understand, and then agree with, my point of view.

    1   2   3   4   5

People who are close to me (and telling the truth) might agree that I try to control people and/or circumstances.

    1   2   3   4   5

If a situation doesn't have the outcome I wished for, I might try to revisit it with others in hopes of getting the results changed.

    1   2   3   4   5

If the outcome of a decision others have made stacks up in a way that upsets me, I tend to dwell on it rather than move on.

    1   2   3   4   5

I enjoy being in charge and making decisions and policies, especially in my family.

    1   2   3   4   5

I use words carefully to sway others' opinions and conclusions.

    1   2   3   4   5

I attempt to evoke emotions from people to get them to think or feel a certain way so it might get me what I want.

    1   2   3   4   5

I'm told I am pushy, bossy, or controlling.

    1   2   3   4   5

Let's be truthful. I like to get my own way.

    1   2   3   4   5

Now, add up your total. How did you fare?

10–20: You most likely don't have major control issues. Wrap up this book and give it to a bossy friend.

21–30: You vacillate between being agreeable and easygoing at times and, in some situations, wanting to take charge.

31–40: You border on being manipulative. There are certain areas in your life where you pull out the stops to get your way. Better watch it!

41–50: Control-freak alert! Your strength has developed into a weakness and sent others running for cover. Time to stop tweaking and start trusting before all your friends and family scatter for good, and you end up a prisoner of your own pushy self! (Don't feel bad. I scored a 46!)

CHAPTER 2
Our Clamoring Culture

[When I was] a child, my family's menu consisted of two choices:
take it or leave it.
Buddy Hackett

My words are plain to anyone with understanding,
    clear to those with knowledge.
Choose my instruction rather than silver,
    and knowledge rather than pure gold.
For wisdom is far more valuable than rubies.
    Nothing you desire can compare with it.
Proverbs 8:9 – 11 (NLT)

Have you ever secretly wished you lived in a simpler decade in history, perhaps one that didn't demand so much of your time, your energy, your money, or your choices? In other words, a time when you had fewer things you felt you *could* control?

When our children were young, they loved for me to read aloud to them each afternoon before naptime. Since we were homeschooling the kids, even as an elementary school student, Mackenzie, our oldest, could still join in on the read-aloud session each afternoon when the boys were toddlers and preschoolers.

Her favorite books were from the Little House series made famous by American author Laura Ingalls Wilder. Mackenzie completely identified with the main character and her dangling brown braids, a gingham bonnet strung down her back, and her accompanying spunky attitude. In fact, Mackenzie would often don her own blue-flowered bonnet, a present from her antique-loving Grandma Shug, and with her matching auburn braids swaying as she played, would refuse to answer when I called for her, unless of course I addressed her as Laura or Half-Pint. There were days she was so in character when exploring our suburban backyard-turned-imaginary-prairie, that I think she actually believed she *was* Laura Ingalls.

Yes, my little lass fell in love with the era of the late 1870s, the time in which the heroine of the Little House books lived. She adored the stories of the simple one-room schoolhouses, the girls' fancy Sunday-go-to-meetin' dresses, and the always-amusing antics of the rurally raised siblings.

As my own Half-Pint became enamored with this culture, I too began to dream of yesteryears gone by. I grew to love the pictures Wilder painted on my mind's canvas of brightly colored jars of fruit jams and canned creations sparkling as they cooled on the counter, the sunlight dancing through the crystal-clear glass. Her description of Ma's fresh bread emerging from the oven made my mouth water and made me want to take up baking whole wheat bread from scratch. (Yep. I did. I even bought a wheat grinder.)

Ma Ingalls was a busy, industrious woman. There were many laborious farm chores for women of this era to perform. And there were manual as well as mental efforts that a prairie homemaker had to exert. Even though I knew Ma's daily existence wasn't a walk in the park (I may have a broken washing machine, but I've managed to avoid grasshopper plagues), there was something about it that intrigued me. What was it?

Simplicity. Pure simplicity that resulted from a lack of choices.

Life was hard in the late-nineteenth century for women such as dear Ma, but it seems they accepted the difficulties more readily. After all, they knew they couldn't change the weather, totally avoid disease and pestilence, or even change their surroundings with ease. We, however, have the illusion of control. We think that with the snap of a finger or the click of a mouse, we can change situations and create happiness. The truth is, we can't.

Variety Overload

Today's woman has before her infinite choices throughout the course of her day. When packing lunches for her kids, she can choose lunch meat, leftovers, or good old peanut butter and jelly. If she goes with the deli-meat choice, dozens of types of meat await her at the grocers' counter. If she settles on turkey, then she still needs to choose a brand. Once the brand is selected, then her brain must process the next step — sliced or shaved. And if shaved, well, then, how thinly?

If the lunch-meat decision overwhelms her, this woman can choose simple and go with the peanut butter option instead. But while choosy mothers may choose Jif, the rest of us may stand in the aisles flabbergasted, not knowing which jar to select because of brand-name overload.

In fact, my small-town grocery store has no less than eleven different peanut butter brand names proudly perched on its shelves. Multiply that by two, since each brand makes both a creamy and a crunchy variety. (A few even offer extra crunchy for the nuttiest among us!) Then don't forget to count the organic varieties in the health-food section and the reduced-fat styles. Combine these with the many generic and store brands out in grocery land, and you have more peanut butter selections than you can envision for the humble lunch-box sandwich.

You know what Laura Ingalls took in her lunch pail each day? Anything that was left over from the family's last meal. Ma didn't venture off to town to Oleson's Mercantile for some prepackaged fare—à la pricey juice boxes and yummy, individually wrapped granola bars.

And when Ma planned supper for the family each night, she relied on what was within her reach. She had the meat Pa shot on his hunting excursions to bake, fry, or roast for the main dish. She could also utilize whatever fruits or veggies were in season (or the ones she could bring up from the root cellar).

She wasn't like us, for whom choice overload is a daily reality. We can make almost any dish each night, no matter the season, with just a swift trip to the nearby supermarket. If we decide that meat loaf will be tonight's mainstay, a quick Internet search will give us a million different recipes from which to select. And it will present that pertinent info to us in less than a second (along with the choice of whether to search for *meat loaf* or *meatloaf*)!

I'll bet Ma Ingalls owned only one cookbook, if that. Most of her recipes were probably tucked neatly in her bonnet-wearin' noggin.

And it wasn't just in the kitchen where simplicity ruled in the life of a prairie woman.

She probably didn't have one side of the closet reserved for her skinny jeans and the other side for when she'd packed on a few too many pounds. Her cotton dresses could accommodate a slight flux in her womanly waistline.

She didn't stress over which shade of paint to use in each room of their log home. Or whether the new throw pillows were a good match for the old sofa. (And then debate whether she should return them to Target in the morning and get the sage-green ones instead.) She had no picture poses to decide on for the annual family Christmas card. No signature font style and color to select for her email signature.

Speaking of emails, how about this one? No media clamoring for her attention each day. No TV, computer, phone, or radio. Instead, she quietly hummed hymns to herself as she went about her day.

She had no need to fear that Pa had been out in the corporate world surrounded by gorgeous and capable women with whom she felt she just couldn't compare. He spent his days out in the hot fields, continually staring at the big back end of an ox as he plowed and planted. In comparison, when he returned home each night, Ma would look mighty fine to him, even without a stylish haircut or fancy Hollywood makeup. Pa's only vocational choice worked to her advantage here.

Back when women had fewer choices, they didn't have all the opportunities to overcontrol that we do today. Sure, technological and cultural advances present us with boundless inventions and thrilling discoveries. They're supposed to make our lives richer, easier, and more desirable, but do they?

Ma Ingalls, Meet Jane Jetson

When I was a grade-schooler, my older brother and I faithfully watched the Saturday-morning cartoon *The Jetsons*. Set many years in the distant future, the year 2062 to be precise, the futuristic family consisted of father George, homemaker-mom Jane, teenybopper Judy, and boy Elroy, along with faithful family pet Astro (whose every word began with a growling *rrrr* sound even years before the appearance of the infamous *rut-ro* cartoon-canine Scooby-Doo). The way-cool lifestyle of this clan fascinated me. While it was amusing to follow

Wilma and Fred Flintstone back to the Stone Age, it was even cooler to peek into the future with the ultramodern Jetson family.

Just think, my young mind reasoned. *Being able to travel around on people-moving conveyor belts to get places, leaving your deepest secrets in a digital diary, having a family maid that is a bona fide robot, and even flying place to place in zooming spaceships!* It woulda turned Ma Ingalls's Sunday-best bonnet completely inside out.

My imagination soared as I dreamed about my life far off in the future to the year 2000. I even whipped out a piece of paper and a pencil (I didn't own a calculator yet) and figured out how old I would be when that fateful year finally came.

Thirty-five. The same age as Jane Jetson. (Yes, Ma Jetson disclosed her age to the world in the first episode!)

Thirty-five. It seemed so "old lady" and ancient to me.

Little did my second-grade self know that once I passed the "old lady and ancient" mark, I'd look back to my Jetson-watching days with longing — longing for the simple days of only three television stations from which to choose (unless the weather was *just* right and the wind carrying in the proper direction; then we could sometimes get Michigan State University's public television station too). A time without the constant interruptions of cell phones and email notifications that chime and beep, beckoning me away from the people with whom I'm presently sitting and connecting me instantaneously with others who are far away and yet somehow need our urgent attention.

Yes, the period of the 1970s and '80s — dangling smack-dab somewhere in between Caroline Ingalls and Jane Jetson — was the world in which I came of age, an era eager for progress but still somewhat nostalgic about family, faith, and what matters most.

I really miss it. *Sigh*.

Now, in our current culture, although we aren't exactly all jetting about in our own personal spacecrafts (make mine aqua with a bubble-gum-pink Saturn ring for trim, please), we do have some modern trinkets and tools that almost smack of gadgety George and his crew.

Why, just a moment ago, I took a break from my writing nook here at a lovely west Michigan bed-and-breakfast to pop some popcorn, grab a soda, and visit for a minute with Cheri, the proprietor of the inn. When she discovered I was a writer, she asked if I had a digital voice recorder (reminiscent of Judy's digital diary, perhaps?). She said the model she owns can, after recording your voice, be connected to a computer and then make the computer automatically type out what you said. No need to sit in front of a screen to write. You could be driving down the interstate while "writing" your book or blog post at the very same time.

Jumpin' Jetsons, that's astonishing! (Humor me, please. I'm usually a bit behind the curve on techie stuff. I was the last in my circle of friends to own a DVD player and get a cell phone, and I still don't know if I totally comprehend the difference between a PDA and a PDF. I'm sure this voice-recording thingy isn't cutting-edge, brand-spankin' new, but I'd never heard of it.)

This new invention just might help me get more done in less time, although I'm not too keen on verbally blogging while I drive. But while I fold laundry or do dishes or wait in the car during an unplanned long and rainy football practice? Sign me up, sister!

But what might happen if I were to meander on down to the big city, where the Gadgets Galore superstore is, to hunt for this time-saving, handheld companion? Well, I'd find it all right. Probably in scads of different model types. All lined up neatly in rigid rows next to all of its chrome-colored, button-laded, beeping kin.

Smartphones.

Smarter laptops.

Wireless tablets ready to roll.

Bluetooth devices ready to connect.

Personal video-gaming systems.

And on and on it goes!

Even though some of these current inventions might make my life easier, they also demand that I make decisions. I must research. And comparison shop. And finally I must choose. Like standing in the peanut butter–laden aisle of my grocer's, again my mind begins to swirl.

So many options. And since I want to control what model gadgets I'll garner, well, here I come full circle again. I'm forced to control, to choose, to decide. It takes time. It creates even more decisions and more errands. It can consume a large part of my day, a day when I'm already being pulled in so many directions. Simply because I live in a land chock-full of choices!

I'd even assert that our menagerie of selections, and their accompanying commitments, seeks to chip away at our patience, gobble up our brain space, and erode our enjoyment. Instead of making our lives easier and simpler, these inventions, discoveries, and opportunities can actually make life harder and more complicated. They give us many, many opportunities to control things, when what we really need is a guide who will lead us *past* our need to control.

What's Your Plumb Line?

Have you ever read through the Gospels and noticed how Jesus didn't seem to get rattled by the stuff that rattles us? He didn't seem bothered by busyness, distracted by decisions, or particularly perturbed by people (well, except maybe those persnickety and pious Pharisees. But even then he spoke the truth and moved on rather than dwell on them and their bad behavior). The Lord's ability to interact with others, live his life intentionally, and fulfill his mission in an unruffled and focused manner both inspires and intrigues me.

All around him, people were beckoning for him to do something. His twelve closest friends, the rough and tumble disciples, needed him to feed the gathering crowd. They didn't have any idea how to pull off a catered affair for five thousand tired and hungry folks in the middle of a hot and dusty day on a huge hillside.

Random citizens on the street begged him to alter his intended course and go heal their ailing relatives. Others wanted to press in close to him for a glance, a touch, or a word. It seems that everywhere Jesus went, people needed him and pronto! But somehow the clamor and clutching didn't unnerve him and knock him off course. Why?

Because Jesus had a plumb line.

Here's what I'm talking about: When Todd and I bought our first home, the walls in the kitchen were in such dire shape that they couldn't be painted. They were peppered with bumps and gouges and numerous flaws from their forty years of existence. Their only hope for decorating redemption was to get covered by wallpaper and a hefty layer of underwear.

You read that right. That's what the smooth-talking salesman down at the local paint store called the long rolls of white, thick, tightly woven fiber that was to be put on the wall before my friend Michelle and I could tackle adhering the wallpaper. This nifty product promised to cover the wall's secret sins.

I selected a fancy-pants pattern from the half-dozen books at the store (can't imagine how many in-person and online choices there'd be out there today). The pattern I chose had a stripe in it (what was I thinking?), so it was crucial that we create a plumb line before starting. Otherwise, the wallpaper might get put up crooked. If we tried lining up the paper with the wall's edge without checking to see whether the walls were right-angle straight and level, then if the walls were cockeyed, the wallpaper would be applied off-kilter too, and it would be horribly noticeable, especially in the bold, banded pattern I'd picked.

So Michelle taught me how to make a plumb line. We started with a winding reel of thick thread that was rigged in such a way that the thread was coated with a bright-blue chalk powder as it came out of the spool. On the end of the woven thread was a small, acorn-sized, grey metal weight.

Michelle stood on a ladder. I stayed happily on the ground. She snugged the spool up to the top of one corner of my retro-but-soon-to-be-modern kitchen and dropped the chalk-covered line. After waiting for the metal weight to stop its pendulum-like, rhythmic swaying, she told me to hold it tight and taut up to the bottom of the wall where it nearly touched the floor.

Then *snap!* she gave the sturdy string a good pluck as if playing a giant bass guitar, and it magically marked the wall with a bright blue line that was perfectly vertical. We used that thin streak as our plumb line and starting point when we lined up the edge of our first strip of wallpaper. At the end of the day, our finished product was neatly and squarely applied. Without that plumb line, the wallpaper would have leaned sideways like the Tower of Pisa, making me dizzy every time I cooked in the kitchen.

As Jesus went through his earthly life, he had a plumb line—a solid starting point of reference on which he based all of his decisions. It was straightforward and uncomplicated: he came to do his Father's will by glorifying him while on earth (John 17:1).

He was intentional about spending time alone with God in prayer, knitting his heart to the Father's so they were united in purpose. Then, whenever he was faced with a choice, he first sifted it through the grid of glory. He didn't think, *Will this glorify me?* He pondered, *Will this glorify God?* If it wouldn't, he didn't do it. If it would, he proceeded with confidence. He understood his mission on earth and had a proper perspective on who he was. And who he wasn't.

In John 8, we find the Lord chatting with some of the Jews. They wanted to know who he really was after hearing his claims that someone who believed in him would never see death. Did he think he was greater than Abraham? Than the prophets? Just where did Jesus put himself on the spiritual spectrum of popularity?

When answering them, Jesus humbly declared, "If I glorify myself, my glory means nothing" (John 8:54). He, as the Son of God, had the right perspective on what (and who) our lives should be all about. He knew who should control our choices and who gets the credit for us making the right ones.

Cat and Dog Theology

When I became a follower of Christ late in high school, I first encountered the expression "glorify God." It was a theological term, and I guessed from how I heard it dangling in some

Christians' sentences, that it was equivalent to the phrase "please God." Well, I've since learned that's only the half of it.

A friend of mine told me about a seminar that came to her church called Unveiling Glory. It had revolutionized how she processed her relationship with Christ. A few years later, my home church hosted this wonderful conference. There I learned firsthand what her excitement was about.

The word *glorify*, as first used in Old Testament Hebrew, means "to make famous" or "to throw one's weight around." So when we say our actions should glorify God, they should point to him and make him famous to those watching. That was Jesus' plumb line, and it should be ours too. It is best explained by a rather peculiar concept I learned from the people at Unveiling Glory.[1]

Cat and dog theology.

It goes like this: A dog's master comes home at the end of a hard day. The dog heartily greets him at the door, goes all crazy with affection and the occasional slobber, and fetches his owner's slippers. He is thrilled to be in his master's presence and wants to please him. His actions say this: "You love me. You feed me. You scratch my neck and pet my back. You provide for my every need. Wow! You must be God!" (pant, pant, lick, slobber, lick).

A cat, on the other hand, greets her master at the end of the hard day like this: She doesn't budge when she hears her owner come through the door, nor does she bother to get up off her master's favorite chair. She lies there unimpressed, lazily sunning herself in a patch of sunlight, thinking only about herself. With her ambivalent actions, she seems to say this, "You? Oh, are *you* home? Ya know, I was just lounging here thinking about you, and I've finally figured something out. You love me. You feed me. You scratch my neck and pet my back. You provide for my every need. Wow! *I* must be God!"

When we go through life looking out for ourselves, taking control rather than trusting God for guidance, making decisions based solely on what's best for us rather than what will make God most famous to those around us, we're elevating ourselves above God and buying into backward, upside-down cat theology.

Bad kitty!

Because Jesus' plumb line was to give God the glory and not snatch it for himself, he properly made God famous. And by doing so, he could avoid decision overload.

He made the ultimate, big-picture decision to bring God glory. Consequently, the little day-to-day decisions didn't fluster him but instead fell neatly into place. He always referred back to his original measuring stick — "Will this bring my Father glory?" Because he wisely exerted ultimate control over what he allowed to be his plumb line, he didn't need to over-control dozens of minor, time- and energy-wasting decisions. Each person's request, each time he rested or preached, each conversation he engaged in — he ran it all through the grid of his Father's glory.

Tool, Toy, or Tangent

I love the plumb line of doing life for God's glory. But at times *glory* can still feel like a lofty term. So I've learned to ask myself a question, in the midst of this clamoring culture, that helps me decide what will glorify God and, in the end, somehow please me too. (I've found that striving to please myself often ends up doing the exact opposite. But you can't ever go wrong when you aim to please God.)

So when it comes to a purchase, an activity, an event, a friendship, a hobby, or a pastime, I ask myself, "Is this a tool, a toy, or a tangent?"

Tools are needed. They help us live life. They enable us to take care of our homes and families. They help us grow physically, emotionally, and spiritually. Nothing wrong with tools.

Toys are permissible too. We all need a little fun now and then to help us relieve stress and rejuvenate, to refresh our minds, bodies, and souls. I love me a good toy now and then.

It's the tangents that trip us up—those activities, hobbies, people, or time-wasting habits that knock us off course for an hour. Or a year.

Take social media, for example. We can utilize Facebook and Twitter as tools to keep up with our extended families, or even family members nearby. (Yes, I've sent my child a Facebook message before, summoning him to supper when he was in my house but on another floor!) We can use Instagram to share and receive prayer requests, to advertise a business or grow a ministry. Social media can be an effective tool.

It can also be a toy. If on Facebook you want to plant your rows of squash and harvest your sweet corn or have yourself a nifty little Mafia war (sounds kinda violent to me), you go right ahead. Have a blast! Just please don't ask me to join you. Those games and challenges would not relax me. They'd stress me out. I'm still looking for the "block all requests that aren't conversations I want to have, parties I want to attend, or causes that I want to give to" button. Yes, Facebook as an occasional toy is great.

Where we get into trouble is when social media crosses the line and turns into a tangent. Who hasn't been sucked into the black hole of social media a time or two? You sit down to check your home page and see what the rest of Facebook land is up to.

Two hours and hundreds of clicks later, you realize you've been frittering and twittering your time away, with no worthwhile purpose. *Tangent Warning!*

To keep social media from zipping from tool to tangent in less time than it takes to say "Mark Zuckerberg," you'll need to come up with some big-picture control guidelines. These will help you keep from spinning out of control and then being faced with another whole slew of unwanted choices in this media-saturated culture. (Yes, each click brings more choices. So stop clicking already!)

You might consider putting in place some guidelines like these:

- I will only check Facebook twice a day.

- When I check it, I'll also check the clock and limit myself to fifteen minutes.

- I'll make sure I'm not friends with anyone who will pull me in a wrong direction morally, anyone from my past whom I feel uncomfortable having in my life, or anyone with whom my spouse feels uneasy about me connecting.

- With friends whose status updates make me either feel left out, angry, or upset, I'll hide their news feed so it doesn't come up on my page. (They won't know you did this, and you'll still be Facebook "friends.")

- During my time on Facebook, I'll mentally ask myself, "Right now, is this a tool, a toy, or a tangent?"

- If I ever feel that this activity is overshadowing my time in actual face-to-face relationships with my family or getting in the way of my relationship with God, I'll declare a Facebook fast and won't go back until it no longer is a stronghold in my life.

Social media is just one area where deliberate simplification may be needed to help you maintain perspective and not wander off into tangent land. There are many other parts of your life where it might be helpful to apply some big-picture control guidelines that will allow the smaller decisions to take care of themselves. Here are some examples:

where you shop

how you dress

what you own

how you eat

where you vacation

with whom you hang out

where you serve and volunteer

what activities and sports your kids take part in

what kinds of media you allow into your family's life

When boundaries and guidelines are in place for your family, you don't need to constantly overcontrol with harping and reminding and correcting. You just calmly point your kids (or yourself!) to the overarching big-picture boundary.

Yes, this is actually a call to control — in order to avoid overcontrol! It's a call to make larger, overarching decisions so the smaller decisions will take care of themselves *or be deliberately and actively ignored.*

Just as Jesus' life was about obedience to God, love of others, and service, so should ours. So we must intentionally put in place guidelines that will help us maintain the proper perspective and, like Jesus, keep our mission ever in sight. As a result, we end up glorifying God and making him famous, not just feeding our own wishes and desires and controlling people and circumstances to our liking while we attempt to exist in our crazy-busy, clamoring culture.

It's about Time

If time transport were possible, maybe I'd whisk myself back to Ma Ingalls's era on the American prairie in the 1870s and ask her the secret to her flaky piecrust. Or I'd catapult forward into the future and catch a flying-saucer ride with Jane Jetson, circa 2062. (Hey, that doesn't seem so far off now. I don't need a new-fangled calculator to tell me I'd be ninety-eight years old if I lived that long!)

Alas, I had no say about the time period for my sojourn on the earth. Neither did you. But no matter the era we roam our streets and sidewalks, our mission is the same. Obey God. Love and serve others. And do it with a smile so that the watching world will want to know more about the God we faithfully serve as we glorify him with our choices.

To be effective during our time here on earth, we must each learn to discern and decide just what our big-picture plumb line is. We must weed through the many offerings presenting themselves to us to discover our unique niche in the overall mission that will enable us to glorify God. Then we'll be positioned to maintain our perspective as life comes at us full speed. We'll learn to listen for God's voice amid the clamor of our culture, and we'll discover how we can control what we should and trust God with all the rest.

Oh, and how to make him *way* famous in the process by exhibiting to others our proper doglike theology.

As Astro would say, "Ruff, ruff!"

Other Relevant Tangents

Facebook is just one black hole that can siphon away your time, leaving you distracted and inefficient. Other areas in your life can knock you off course and tempt you to spend oodles of hours on a tangent. Remember, if something is a tool, great! And if it's a temporary toy to help you relax, that's fine too. But watch for the all-out tangent — something that doesn't prove to be helpful, useful, or relaxing but rivets your attention onto the trivial and pulls you away from the important. See if any of the following areas, though not wrong in and of themselves, might rear up in your life as a tangent if given to excess:

- engaging in a hobby, such as scrapbooking, or a pastime that requires equipment or maintenance, such as horseback riding, gardening, motorcycling, or owning a hot tub or built-in pool
- watching television — from morning talk shows to after noon soaps to evening reality TV
- reading fiction novels
- watching movies
- talking on the phone
- cruising the cyber superhighway looking at websites
- reading daily blogs
- tuning in to home-shopping networks on TV (that can take both our time *and* our money!)
- exercising
- participating in a sport or music group
- shopping for leisure rather than need
- daydreaming
- cleaning (Yes, there is such a thing as overcleaning!)
- spending time with friends

Remember, most of these things may be fine in and of themselves (not the soap operas, by the way). Only you can truly tell when your attention to them has crossed the line and now turned into a tangent.

To recognize a tangent, see if you would answer yes to any of the following questions:

1. When you're through with the activity and peek at the clock, are you shocked at how much time passed while you were doing it?

2. When you're not participating in the activity, do you still think about it?

3. In between times, do you wonder if others are participating in the activity and feel a bit left out?

4. When you're not engaged in the activity, do you plot and plan when to do it again?

5. Has either of these thoughts ever crossed your mind: *I really spend too much time doing this* or *I can't seem to go a day without participating in this activity*?

6. Do you feel any sense of guilt when you've spent a great deal of time in the activity and worry that you're neglecting something else you should be doing, whether at work or at home?

Please note: I am not talking about passions here, not ministry or service-oriented activities. I'm referring to an obsessive, unproductive, or trivial focus on a seemingly innocent hobby or pastime.

The best method for attacking and eliminating tangents is to put some accountability in place. Have a close friend hold you accountable. Have her call you to ask about your tangents and see if you have overparticipated in them. Pick someone who will hold you to your goals but will also have a gracious and gentle attitude so you'll feel free to be honest with her. Also, be sure to give yourself grace as you change your behavior patterns. Some tangents' roots run deep, and weeding them out of your life may be thorny and tedious. Give yourself time. Look for progress, not perfection.

CHAPTER 3

The Seduction of Self

I am the master of my fate: I am the captain of my soul.
William Ernest Henley

Many are the plans in a person's heart
but it is the LORD's purpose that prevails.
Proverbs 19:21

All Wanda Holloway wanted was for her daughter to be happy. And absolutely nothing would make thirteen-year-old daughter, Shanna, shriek with delight more than to land a spot on the award-winning high school cheerleading team from Channelview, Texas.

So what did the concerned mom from the Lone Star State do? Encourage her daughter to exert her best effort? To perfect a strong and loud chanting voice? To solidly land her jumps, flowingly turn her cartwheels, and repeatedly rehearse her arm motions until she was considered a top contender for a coveted spot on the spirited squad?

Nope.

Did she hire a personal coach — someone well versed in the skills and drills of competitive cheerleading who could help her offspring effectively train for the day of the big audition?

Uh-uh.

Perhaps she asked an older squad member to work with young Shanna, drawing upon her experience to give pointers that would make a positive difference in Shanna's performance, enabling her to confidently appear before the scrutinizing panel of judges and thus be chosen for the lineup?

No, ma'am.

This determined suburban mom went further. Much, much further.

To ensure her daughter's happiness, Wanda Holloway decided to hire a hit man.

Yes, a hit man, as in someone who willingly kills for a lump sum of cash. She sought out a gentleman (term loosely used, mind you) who agreed to murder the mother of Shanna's classmate and competitor Amber Heath.

The price tag? Twenty-five hundred dollars.

The payoff? Shanna would be a cheerleader at last. After all, she had been cut from the squad the prior two years, and her meddling mother deemed that rival Amber Heath was the cause. Amber had snatched up a spot from Wanda's sweet Shanna and was the one cheering happily on the sidelines while Shanna sat, dejected, in the stadium bleachers, just another commoner in the crowd. Yes, Wanda determined it was time her baby girl had a turn at the perpetual popularity that often accompanies pom-pom-toting Texan teens.

Wanda's skewed line of thinking was this: Amber would be so utterly distraught at the death of her mother that she'd drop out of the running. Or if she did audition, she'd certainly not compete at her best, ensuring a subpar performance. The result would be failure to make the squad. Either scenario, Wanda surmised, would pave the way for Shanna to outshine her rival. Her daughter would then receive the desirable right to don a Channelview High School cheerleading uniform the next school year, her very important and impressionable first year of senior high.

Thankfully, the conniving housewife's plan was foiled. Instead of ensuring her daughter's high school happiness, the stupid stunt got Ms. Holloway a do-not-pass-go, all-expenses-paid ticket to a Texas prison.

The irony? Rival Amber Heath's mom, Verna, the object of the assassination plot, declared that Shanna most likely would have made the cheerleading squad anyway. She really needed no help from her mother—other than the usual verbal support and occasional homemade snacks most moms give their kids when they pursue an extracurricular endeavor.

Instead, the obsessed maternal (and now criminal) character's choices secured her fifteen minutes of shame in twentieth-century American tabloid history. She became notorious for her runaway desire to control people and her no-holds-barred attempt to affect the outcome of a situation to her liking.

Perhaps it wasn't so much about a mom's all-out attempt to secure something her daughter coveted. Maybe it was more about a woman wanting something for herself—to be the mother of a high school cheerleader. And she would go to any length to see that selfish scenario play out on the real screen of her life.

At least *we* aren't like Wanda Holloway.

Or are we?

Let's find out.

Gardening 101

Have you ever really pondered the person of Eve? I mean more than our childhood mental picture of Eve's flowing hair, strategically placed in such a way that our young minds knew she was naked. (In my neck of the woods, *naked* means you have no clothing on. *Neckid* means you have no clothing on, and you're

47

up to something.) Thankfully, the children's Bible illustrator made certain our elementary-school-age eyes spied only Eve's peeking appendages and cheery, contented face as she sat parked on the page smack-dab in the center of Eden National Park.

Flip forward a few pages in your mind to retrieve the next snapshot of the account. Enter Satan, in the form of a snake. The plot thickens as Paradise is about to be spoiled because Sister Eve decided one day that she wanted to have more control.

Let's plop ourselves into the Bible's account located in Genesis 3, reprinted here in the New Living Translation (italics added for emphasis):

> The serpent was the shrewdest of all the wild animals the LORD God had made. One day he asked the woman, "Did God *really* say you must not eat the fruit from any of the trees in the garden?" (verse 1)

Step one: Satan hissed, hurling doubt Eve's way and causing her to second-guess God's plan and to question his commands. Eve was easily sucked into the serpent's trap:

> "Of course we may eat fruit from the trees in the garden," the woman replied. "It's only the fruit from the tree in the middle of the garden that we are not allowed to eat. God said, 'You must not eat it *or even touch it*; if you do, you will die.'" (verses 2–3)

Step Two: Eve didn't stay true to God's guidelines. She added a few words to his directive, thereby convoluting the truth of his instructions to her. A chapter earlier, in Genesis 2:16–17, God had clearly stated, "You may freely eat the fruit of every tree in the garden — except the tree of the knowledge of good and evil. If you eat its fruit, you are sure to die." No mention of not touching it. That part dear Eve pulled right out of Paradise's clear blue sky.

Satan knew he had Eve right where he wanted her:

> "You won't die!" the serpent replied to the woman. "God knows that your eyes will be opened as soon as you eat [the fruit], and you will be like God, knowing both good and evil." (verses 4–5)

Step Three: Satan twisted reality. He placed a subtle spin on God's words, not so much to convince Eve (and us) that *he* knew better than God, but that somehow *she* did (and so do we). And the result of Satan's warped little ploy?

> The woman was convinced. She saw that the tree was beautiful and its fruit looked delicious, and she wanted the wisdom it would give her. So she took some of the fruit and ate it. Then she gave some to her husband, who was with her, and he ate it, too. At that moment their eyes were opened, and they suddenly felt shame at their nakedness. So they sewed fig leaves together to cover themselves. (verses 6–7)

Step Four: Eve convinced herself. Ignoring the truth of the Creator's commands, she launched out, crafting her own reality. She fashioned her fate and ours (or so we imagine). She screamed with her attitude and subsequent actions, "I know better than you, God!" And the results were disastrous for the human race.

Just like Eve, we convince ourselves that we are the masters of our own fates, crafting our own realities. We too think we know better than God. And the results are never, ever, *ever* good. We may even, like Eve, entangle others in our webs of self-deceit.

So as not to force poor Eve to take responsibility for the entire fall of humankind, let's not forget Adam's part. Eve offered him a nibble of the forbidden fruit. He could have refused to taste it, but he didn't.

(Note: While oral tradition and painted portraits have suggested the fruit was an apple, many scholars and historians believe it was a grape. Or a pomegranate. Or perhaps a fig—since, upon being caught, Adam and Eve grabbed fig leaves to fashion speedy, naturally organic, yet stylish wardrobes for themselves.

My personal opinion?

It was a deep, dark-chocolate, festive foiled-wrapped, whack-open orange—the kind my hubby hides in the toe of my stocking on Christmas morning. That would have been the only fruit that stood a chance of tempting me!)

Back to our story. Adam wasn't entirely innocent. He chose to accuse. In one single Scripture verse, he cunningly cast a double portion of blame.

> The man replied, "*It was the woman* you gave me who gave me the fruit, and I ate it." (verse 12)

Interpretation: "Uh ... it wasn't me ... It was *that woman*." Scapegoat number one. "It was actually the Mrs. who made me do it. Uh ... and by the way, God ..." Let's run a little instant replay on that verse to point out something else ...

> The man replied, "It was the woman *you gave me* who gave me the fruit, and I ate it." (verse 12)

Further interpretation: "See. It wasn't me. It was the woman. The woman ... *ahem* ... that *you* gave me!"

Here we have the first buck-naked man passing the first buck. He took no ownership in his part of this epic and true tale. He blamed the little lady. And he blamed the Lord himself.

How many times have I ... have you ... done the same? These kids of yours! This situation you have me in! Buck passing at its best, or worst.

Now. Stop for a minute and also consider what a fool Ms. Eve was.

Seriously.

The woman lived in Paradise. With *one* man! She felt no temptation to compare him to Joe the handy hubby or Dave down the street who "always remembers his wife's birthday"!

She'd never faced the pain of an unwanted divorce, the challenges of being a widow, or the frustration of dealing with the sometimes-insensitive things people say to women who are single.

She hadn't been passed over for the promotion, left out of the circle of friends, cut from the cheerleading squad, or booted off the chess team.

No, Eve's life — physically and emotionally — was a breeze. Why, her husband had never even laid eyes upon another woman, let alone any of the airbrushed images that Hollywood cranks out. In his eyes, she was flawless!

God had crafted a perfect plan for her earthly existence. All she needed to do was trust him to reveal it to her and then kick back and enjoy it. And him.

The Creator had even told Eve that she could eat of any of the trees in that beautiful paradise. All except for *that* one.

So Eve, like many of us, looked around at the countless comforts that had been given to her and said, "But I want *that*." And she bought the first and most devastating lie of the Devil, hook, line, and "sink her." Why?

Self.

Today we still buy lies of self from slicker-than-snake-oil Satan. Instead of being grateful for all God *has* given us, we look at our neighbor or our sister-in-law or the gal in the cubicle next to us and announce ... "I'll have what she's having, please."

We never learn. We women, just like Eve, clamor for control, scrap for self, and chase seemingly elusive contentment.

Redefining Reality

Any female who has lived more than a decade is often faced with this harsh and disappointing reality: we women don't always get our way.

Bummer.

Maybe in the delightful fairy tales we read as children or on the air-brushed tabloids we now spy as adults in the grocery-store checkout lane, the heroine of the story not only lives happily ever after but gets to decide just what that "ever after" looks like. But in reality — in grown-up-world, relationship-challenged, sometimes-economic-hard-times or subpar health reality — we are simply not able to call all the shots. While we may strive to better ourselves — to create opportunities or rise to challenges, to be the mistresses of our own destinies — in many ways, we get the life we're given.

The hand we're dealt.

The mismade mocha cappuccino we're served that cannot be remade. (I asked for decaf, not regular!)

End of story.

After more than forty years of being female, I have come to a bold and harsh realization: Someone is always going to rearrange my building blocks. Or move my dolls. Or alter my circumstances. Or disappoint my child. Or mess with my schedule. Or paint a picture of my character, however false. And oftentimes I really have no say in the matter.

So, what are the offspring of Eve to do? Should we fume and fuss? Kick up our shiny stilettos and throw ourselves a major hissy fit? Micromanage and manipulate to get our own way?

No. No. And no.

Believe me, I've tried all of those approaches, and they rarely work. And even if they do work in the short term, they soon come back to nip and gnaw at me.

Our only solution is to cultivate the gentle art of acceptance, of learning not to ask "Why me?" but rather "What am I supposed to learn at this junction of life that will make me a better person and draw me closer to God?" We shouldn't pout, asking God to get us out of the circumstances. Instead of crying, "Lord, get me out of here!" we should instead be praying, "Lord, why have you brought me here?"

When we adopt this line of thinking, we can experience the thrilling feeling of being "out of control" and loving it.

I am so not joking.

I know that with our multitasking, wired-to-be-in-control-and-in-charge-of-ten-things-at-once womanly personalities, this doesn't seem plausible. But I hope through our journey together, you too will discover that in keeping our strengths as strengths (and not letting them shift into troublesome weaknesses) and in living out lives that strive for order but willingly accept God's interruptions, we will find that life can be exhilarating.

So please pause, my reading friend. Take a deep breath. I don't believe it's a coincidence that you're holding this book just now. You and I have much to learn about letting go, about prying our fingers off of the control wheel of life and giving it back to the One who created multitasking, take-charge women in the first place.

Let's purpose together to find our purpose, to willingly play the role *God* has picked out for each of us in the grand stage of life. When we do, we'll be a reflection of his perfection and not of our own fake veneer.

Which would you rather be: a luminous mirror that reflects God and his plan for humankind, or a picture of perfection who is actually on the brink of certain failure, retracing the dangerous steps of both Mother Eve and the wacky Wandas of life, a woman destined for heartache and distant from God?

When we willingly accept our lot in life, welcoming all that God is trying to teach us through it, we lose the drive to over-control, to micromanage in an all-out attempt to appear perfect and ensure everything in our lives is "just so."

Then we can learn to practice the secret cheer of contentment: *Let it go!*

As a result, our nerves will be calmed.

Our stress level will deflate.

Our tasks will be less about work and more about worship.

Our decisions will become easier.

We will experience more joy and be strapped with less worry.

Past experiences will begin to make sense.

Our present will seem more doable.

Our future will actually begin to come into focus.

The pretense of perfection will fade away, and a stunningly striking authenticity will be reflected instead.

Life becomes not about self but all about the Savior.

At last we learn to rest, to trust, to accept. And for some of us, really ascertain for the first time just how to live in God's presence. We begin taking our cues from him rather than listening to deceit and becoming convinced that we know better than God and then calling all the shots ourselves, with no better results than banishment from paradise or a stay in a sterile, cold penitentiary.

Then we, for the first time perhaps, walk by faith, not by sight. Nor by strategy. Nor by plotting and positioning.

Ready to give it a try?

You'll discover it's an exhilarating place — letting go, moment by moment, of the need to control, with self off the throne and bowed at his feet where it belongs.

A Selfishness Switch-er-oo

Whenever I discover a helpful feature in the techie computer world, this learned-to-type-on-an-electric-typewriter gal is thrilled. One of my favorites? Find and replace. It's a feature in my word-processing program that allows me to locate an existing word and exchange it for a more suitable word or phrase.

Let's apply this exercise to our sometimes-selfish line of thinking. When we're tempted to throw ourselves a pity party with only ourselves on the guest list — no one fancies the company of a whiner — let's replace our negative notions with a fresh insight from God's written Word. Here are some "find and replace" examples to help you pull a selfishness switch-er-oo:

When you're tempted to think ...	Be reminded that God says ...

"What about my rights?"	"You must have the same attitude that Christ Jesus had.
	    Though he was God,
	        he did not think of equality with God
	        as something to cling to.
	    Instead, he gave up his divine privileges;
	        he took the humble position of a slave
	        and was born as a human being."
	
	(Philippians 2:5 – 7 NLT)

"If I don't look out for myself, who will?"	"What is the price of five sparrows — two copper coins? Yet God does not forget a single one of them. And the very hairs on your head are all numbered. So don't be afraid; you are more valuable to God than a whole flock of sparrows." (Luke 12:6 – 7 NLT)
"But what about what *I* want?"	"Carefully determine what pleases the Lord." (Ephesians 5:10 NLT)

When you're tempted to think ...	Be reminded that God says ...
"If I don't look out for myself, who will?"	"What is the price of five sparrows — two copper coins? Yet God does not forget a single one of them. And the very hairs on your head are all numbered. So don't be afraid; you are more valuable to God than a whole flock of sparrows." (Luke 12:6–7 NLT)
"You only go around once. Grab all the gusto you can!"	"Anything I wanted, I would take. I denied myself no pleasure. I even found great pleasure in hard work, a reward for all my labors. But as I looked at everything I had worked so hard to accomplish, it was all so meaningless — like chasing the wind. There was nothing really worthwhile anywhere." (Ecclesiastes 2:10–12 NLT)
"I'm entitled to my opinion."	"Don't repay evil for evil. Don't retaliate with insults when people insult you. Instead, pay them back with a blessing. That is what God has called you to do, and he will bless you for it. For the Scriptures say, 'If you want to enjoy life and see many happy days, keep your tongue from speaking evil and your lips from telling lies. Turn away from evil and do good. Search for peace, and work to maintain it.'" (1 Peter 3:9–11 NLT)
"What's in it for me?"	"And whatever you do, in word or deed, do everything in the name of the Lord Jesus, giving thanks to God the Father through him." (Colossians 3:17 ESV)

When you're tempted to think ...	Be reminded that God says ...
"I gotta look out for number one."	"Do nothing from rivalry or conceit, but in humility count others more significant than yourselves. Let each of you look not only to his own interests, but also to the interests of others. Have this mind among yourselves, which is yours in Christ Jesus." (Philippians 2:3–5 ESV)
"Who cares about them? It's all about me."	"For you have been called to live in freedom, my brothers and sisters. But don't use your freedom to satisfy your sinful nature. Instead, use your freedom to serve one another in love." (Galatians 5:13 NLT)

PART 2

Domestic Director or Tin-Pot Dictator?

Running the Show at Home

We women wear many hats. We can be a worker, a wife, a mother, and a friend while also being a daughter, a sister, a church member, and a volunteer. We plan the meals, cook the food, clean the house, do the wash ... and then? Well, we roll up our sleeves and do it all over again! Being responsible for so many other people and in charge of so many tasks can beckon us into the land of overcontrol. Let's venture into four areas where women are most tempted to try to run the show at home instead of quietly and confidently walking in faith.

CHAPTER 4

Managing Your Man

I am the head of my household. And I have my wife's permission to say so.

Spotted on a man's T-shirt

Man does not control his own fate. The women in his life do that for him.

Groucho Marx

A virtuous and worthy wife [earnest and strong in character] is a crowning joy to her husband, but she who makes him ashamed is as rottenness in his bones.

Proverbs 12:4 (AMP)

I thought it was a match made in heaven.

It was fall of 1983. Gail, my best friend from high school, had come for a visit to my small college campus for the weekend. Classes had been in session just a few days, and I was getting back into the swing of dorm life after interning for a summer for the state fire marshal of Michigan. A returning sophomore, I was reconnecting with classmates from the year before as well as meeting some new ones who either were beginning their freshman year or had enrolled as transfer students.

The girls on my floor had been all aflutter about a group of three guys who had transferred in and were living on the Gamma One men's floor in our dorm. Quickly labeled the "Stevensville Three," they all hailed from a quaint village in the southwestern corner of Michigan, along the shore of Lake Michigan.

And best of all, my floormates asserted, all three coeds were total foxes. (Back then, we didn't say "handsome" or "hot." The proper terminology was *foxy!*)

Since our country campus housed only about eight hundred students, new ones always got noticed. Word of this studly trio of fine-looking men sparked like wildfire. And so did the fact that at least two of them were splendidly unattached.

At that point, my only glimpse of the three amigos had been from a distance while I walked back to my room from the student center a few days prior. They had been out in the side yard next to the dorm assembling a wooden loft for one of their rooms. I had yet to have the thrill of a face-to-face encounter with one of the Stevensville Three. When I did, I was gonna see for myself just what all the girly fuss was about.

As Gail and I sat down at a corner table in the cafeteria for lunch that Saturday afternoon, a spot opened up straight across from me and right next to where she was parked. As I picked at my colorful, veggie-laden chef salad (I'd wanted the deep-fried french-cheese sandwich and fries but had a pom-pom outfit to try on soon), I heard a strange voice ask, "Is this seat taken?"

I looked up from my plate, and there standing before me was an auburn-haired male with a chiseled physique; a soft, soothing voice; and the dreamiest eyes I'd ever seen. They were a unique shade of light green that reminded me of the ocean.

Webster could have snapped this man's picture right then and there and placed it alongside *foxy* in its enormous hardcover, red dictionary.

"Nope," uttered Gail, "you can sit there." (I was choking on a cucumber slice and was unable to speak.)

For the next half hour or so, we visited with this stud muffin. (Excuse me. My eighties are showing again.) He told us he was a transfer student from Stevensville (really? I didn't know that—*wink*) and that his name was Todd, which, by the way, means "fox"!

He talked about his conversion to Christianity the year before and his desire to now go into full-time ministry. He was a runner. And a trumpet player. And he loved jazz music. He didn't, however, love school. But he was eager to attend a Christian college so he could soak up all he could about his newfound faith. In fact, he was majoring in philosophy and religion.

As we chatted, Gail got a smirk on her face that would not wipe off. I knew what she was thinking.

I'd not yet had a serious boyfriend in college. As the sports editor of the newspaper and a baseball freak, when it came to guys, I was usually everybody's pal and nobody's gal. But I didn't want a boyfriend solely for the sake of saying I had one, so I was trying to be patient as other classmates were getting serious or even becoming engaged. I wanted to wait for Mr. Right instead of settling for Mr. Right Now. Most of all, I knew he would need to be someone who wanted to serve God with his life, whether in full-time ministry or in the secular marketplace. Well, and of course it wouldn't hurt if he were a little foxy.

Fifteen minutes or so into the conversation, Gail leaned away from the table on the two back legs of her chair so Todd wouldn't see her antics. She pointed horizontally to him and mouthed the words, "He is the one!" She then pointed up to the sky, winked, and declared, "God told me."

I just kept downing my salad, trying not to kick her under the table and send her chair toppling and her lunch tray flying.

We finished our visit and returned our trays to the dish

room. Todd then trekked off to the library to crack the books for his upcoming Gospels and Acts exam. Gail and I went into the city to shop at the mall and grab a single scoop of coconut-fudge ripple at Loud's Ice Cream Parlor. (Hey, I'd had a salad at lunch. I figured my calorie budget would allow for it.)

But later that day, I curled up with my Bible and thought about Todd. I had a funny feeling about this guy. As I turned the pages, I happened upon Romans 8:25: "But if we hope for what we do not yet have, we wait for it patiently."

I'd written notes before in my Bible during chapel, high-lighting a key word or jotting down a thought about a verse that the speaker had unearthed for the audience (much to the dismay of my momma, who felt that it was sacrilegious to write in the Bible). But never, ever had I done what I was about to do.

I took a purple, fine-tipped marker and wrote next to that verse in the margin: "Met Todd. 9/16/83."

The verse in Romans concluded a passage of Scripture that describes the hope of our future glory with God. That day, however, I was hoping for a glorious future with Todd!

A Passive-Aggressive Marriage

Foxy Todd Ehman and I eventually did date. But not for more than a year. Apparently he didn't go back to his dorm room that autumn afternoon, have his own "Aha!" revelation, and promptly jot my name down in his Bible's margin near Genesis 12:19: "Now then, here is your wife. Take her and go!"

What ensued following our introduction that Saturday was a nearly three-year looooong lesson for me in patience. (Which had been my greatest prayer the entire summer before I met Todd: *Lord, teach me to be patient.* Be careful what you pray for, friends!)

Eventually we did walk down the aisle and off into wedded bliss.

Well, sort of.

This "match made in heaven" had to learn to survive nuptial reality here on the earth. And man, was that terrain rocky. It caught me slightly off-guard.

Since Todd was a laid-back, agreeable sort, we'd not had much turmoil in our courtship. When it came time to decide where to go out to eat or what movie to watch, he rarely had a preference. "You pick," he'd quip.

I loved this setup.

Since I was quite verbal and seemed to have a specific opinion on all of these matters, I got my own way most of the time. It was a dating setup that worked to my advantage, and Todd seemed none the worse for it. Even when I would press him, "Are you sure you don't want to pick?" he rarely voiced his choice.

However, when attempting to flesh out this new marriage living in the same tiny apartment, sharing the same tiny silver Volkswagen Rabbit, well, it got rather dicey.

The faucet dripped and I wanted Todd to fix it. He asked me whom he should call. What? The men in my growing-up days could fix a drippy faucet in their sleep. Who was this guy? Maybe if he whipped out his trumpet and cranked out some smooth jazz, he could lull the annoying drips to sleep.

Conflicts came up with one of his relatives. I wanted him to make a phone call and set the matter straight. He suddenly became allergic to our only phone, the curly-corded one that hung on the kitchenette wall.

He obviously had an aversion to decisions. I, on the other hand, demanded they be made. Shoot, I just made them myself while he sat idly by. (Or while he wandered back to the office at church, where he was appreciated and was frequently told what a great job he was doing.)

We soon began verbally hurling at each other what Todd refers to as "flesh balls." As believers we're told to "walk by the Spirit" and not "gratify the desires of the flesh" (Galatians 5:16). Instead, Todd and I sometimes actually wallow in the flesh, stooping down and scooping up a big ole helping of it to hurl our unsuspecting spouse's way.

Our flesh balls varied from week to week, but they usually were centered on two recurring themes. And always, they were aimed carefully and thrown hard.

I wanted him to stop being so indecisive, to step up, make a move, or tell me what he really thought for once.

Todd wanted me to stop being so bossy, to back off, quit pestering him, and leave him alone, instead of backing him into a corner and making him feel stupid.

He was so passive. It made me get aggressive.

I guess you could say we had a passive-aggressive marriage!

Thus began the journey that my college-sweetheart-turned-hubby and I have traveled as we've attempted to find our groove in the dance that is marriage.

At the core of my issue was my desire to control Todd, including his actions and reactions, his decisions and even his thoughts.

At the crux of his hang-up was a lack of confidence in making decisions. And an underlying fear that when he did make one, it would either be the wrong one or not the one I, his decisive wife, would have chosen.

We're not the only married couple who falls into this cadence. Throughout my life I've witnessed it repeatedly. I've seen it in neighbors and down at the local diner. It's smack-dab in the story line of countless popular sitcoms and inherent in the punch lines of many marital jokes. And often, though we as believers should know (and do) better, it's also in our churches.

Why, we can even find it tucked away in the Bible as we peek into the lives of couples there. Let's take a glance now.

Code Adam

Code Adam is named in memory of Adam Walsh, son of John Walsh, host of *America's Most Wanted*. When you hear the phrase "Code Adam" in a department store, it means a child is lost. It's also fitting because the original Adam was the first man who ever lost his way.

Without totally rehashing the scenario of Adam and the Mrs. that we just dissected last chapter, let's rejoin the biblical account to see what the results of their actions were, for them *and* for us.

When Adam lost his way and joined his wife in her devilish plans, they got busted. No amount of fig leaves or finagling secret tree forts in Eden could conceal them from the Almighty.

When he caught them, God didn't give the couple a pass. He uttered no parental "Now don't you two ever do that again. And go straight to bed without any supper. You already ate enough fruit for an eternity."

Uh-uh. The Creator had to deal swiftly and seriously with the mighty mess his creation had just created.

Let's tune in again to Genesis 3:

> Then the LORD God said to the woman, "What is this that you have done?"
>> The woman said, "The serpent deceived me, and I ate."
>> The LORD God said to the serpent,

"Because you have done this,
  cursed are you above all livestock
  and above all beasts of the field;
on your belly you shall go,
  and dust you shall eat
  all the days of your life.
I will put enmity between you and the woman,
  and between your offspring and her offspring;
he shall bruise your head,
  and you shall bruise his heel."

To the woman he said,

"I will surely multiply your pain in childbearing;
  in pain you shall bring forth children.
Your desire shall be for your husband,
  and he shall rule over you."

(verses 13–16 ESV)

Poor serpent. Doomed to slither about on his belly with dust as his only culinary option. And he was about to encounter a never-ending brawl with the human race, packed with striking and bruising and other not-so-nice goings-on.

Satan, in serpent form, got his marching orders for the rest of eternity from the God of the universe that day. The message was loud and clear: "Don't mess with the Almighty."

Satan's punishment I understood. It was God's words to Eve that puzzled me the first time I really paid attention to them during a college Bible class.

He said he'd multiply her pain in childbearing. I'd been around enough moms and caught wind of their birth stories to know that a lot of pain is involved in birthing a baby. In fact, I sometimes chuckle at the ways women swap birth stories like men swap hunting stories. In one room the guys are one-upping each other about how many points were on the antler rack of the deer they shot. In the other room, the gals are outdoing each other with the length of the horrific transition phase of their labor or how long they had to push before the baby popped out. (Or if you're my friend Jean, an avid hunter, you can participate in both conversations!)

Yes, childbirth involves pain. Even mothers who became so by adoption have experienced pain — the pain of infertility, of waiting, of feeling "less than." Biological moms may have stretch marks to prove they gave birth, but adoptive moms have their hearts stretched as they wait for that final call to come from the adoption agency.

The painful childbirth lingo God used with Eve didn't puzzle me. What perplexed me in Eve's penalty pronouncement from God was the very last sentence: "Your desire shall be for your husband, and he shall rule over you."

Whenever I'd read or heard that verse before, it never made sense. It sounded like Eve would desire her husband — as in think he was foxy, want his bod, and so on. How was that a punishment? The "he shall rule over you" phrase made sense as a penalty. Who likes to be ruled over by another? Certainly not me! But why was it coupled with that whole desiring-your-dude business?

It wasn't until a chapel speaker at college unpacked the Hebrew meaning of this sentence that any lightbulb went off in my Bible-searching brain.

Here's what I learned: In the original Hebrew, the phrase that is translated "Your desire shall be for your husband" actually means that a woman's desire would be for her husband's *position*. Meaning, he would be the pants wearer in the family, but she would want to wiggle her sweet little self into them instead and leave him holding a fig leaf. When I strung those two thought patterns together, the mysterious Scripture verse finally made sense.

As a woman you'll desire to be the boss, but your husband has already been assigned that job description.

Bummer.

I know, I know. Many gals insist, "But my husband isn't the spiritual leader of our family." My heart goes out to you, but I must disagree. He is the leader, by virtue of his office. Whether he's doing his job or not is up for debate. One can hold an office or title and refuse to fulfill the duties of that office.

The New Living Translation actually spells out this concept a bit more clearly for us in its rendering of Genesis 3:16: "You will desire to control your husband, but he will rule over you."

Controlling our husbands is as old as the hills. The hills of Eden, that is.

Of course the other half of the curse is no prettier. No one likes a controlling wife with a passive hubby, but a domineering husband and an overly submissive wife is just as bad.

So what is the solution to this domestic dilemma? Are we simply left to duke it out for control in our marriages? Or do we just adopt a woman-take-charge, man-head-for-the-recliner setup where she wears the pants and he wears the "Yes, dear" T-shirt? Is this the best, *or even the biblical*, approach?

Where does our answer lie?

Time to hit the dance floor.

Dancing with the "Ours"

This is where I fear I may lose some of you. The topic of husband-wife roles in the Bible and the accompanying dreaded S word — *submission* — is very polarizing. Some of you may even skip this section, since you can sense I'm gonna use the S word, and you don't care to hear it. You believe it's an antiquated term that no longer applies to marriages today, a cultural term the apostle Paul used that is null and void in the twenty-first century.

I know there are parts of the Bible that are hard to wrap our brains around. I get that. But I also know that each and every word is "God-breathed" and able to teach, correct, rebuke, and train us for righteousness (2 Timothy 3:16). So I can't just wield a Sharpie marker and black out the verses that make me bristle a bit or go against my human (and sinful) nature.

On the other end of the spectrum, I fear I may scare off some sisters with my explanation of biblical marriage as I see it, since I'm about to refer to it in terms of dancing. Some of you think dancing is plain wrong, so you'll have nothing to do with it, even as an analogy in a book.

In my mind, I believe there are right and wrong ways to dance. There are suggestive and smutty dances. Or old-fashioned hokey-pokey lines danced at weddings or the swing-your-partner-round-and-round dances of a harvest-time hoedown. But if you really believe all dancing is forbidden and evil, you must grab that Sharpie and black out portions of the Bible.

I pray that if you fall into either of these categories, you'll humor me just until the end of this chapter. Pretty please? Okay, so—hang with me now—let's talk the marriage two-step.

Ballroom dancing, when done by experts, can be beautiful to watch. The dancers swirl and twirl, sway and dip as they appear to glide effortlessly across the wood floor floating in perfect unison. At times the dance travels toward the girl. Then the direction changes, and it migrates back to the man's side of the floor. No matter the direction the couple moves, one thing is certain.

For the dance to fall into place, the woman must follow the man's lead.

It doesn't mean she's inferior or less than or subservient. It isn't about importance. It's about function and roles. If the end result — a smooth and breathtaking dance — is desired, there are no two ways around it: the gal must follow her partner's lead.

I see marriage very much in this way.

In trying to understand the New Testament passages that speak of husbands and wives and the S word (Ephesians 5 and Colossians 3), I think Satan slithers back in and attempts to say again to today's modern woman, "Did God *really* say ...?" He wants to trick, convolute, and confuse.

Here's how these portions of Scripture read in the Amplified Version, which expounds upon the original intent of the language in which the words were first penned, in this case Greek:

> Wives, be subject to your husbands [subordinate and adapt yourselves to them], as is right and fitting and your proper duty in the Lord. Husbands, love your wives [be affectionate and sympathetic with them] and do not be harsh or bitter or resentful toward them. (Colossians 3:18 – 19)

Ephesians 5:22 – 27 echoes this:

> Wives, be subject (be submissive and adapt yourselves) to your own husbands as [a service] to the Lord. For the husband is head of the wife as Christ is the Head of the church, Himself the Savior of [His] body. As the church is subject to Christ, so let wives also be subject in everything to their husbands.
>
> Husbands, love your wives, as Christ loved the church and gave Himself up for her, so that He might sanctify her, having cleansed her by the washing of water with the Word, that He

might present the church to Himself in glorious splendor, without spot or wrinkle or any such things [that she might be holy and faultless].

These marriage passages might help each of us find our own unique groove. You see, there is no cookie-cutter design for Christian marriages. I've seen more confusion, finger pointing, and condemnation heaped upon wives by well-meaning Christians who have adopted Famous Christian Brother So-and-So's ninety-five principles for marriage or parenting or whatever. They pull some of these principles right out of the air and then not only treat them as scriptural commands but heap guilt upon others who don't also follow dear Brother So-and-So's ways.

And so many well-meaning believers who want desperately to fit into the social circle of the rule followers feel controlled by peer pressure. They, in turn, begin to exert immense control, making sure their lives (and their kids' lives) fall perfectly in line with all ninety-five principles.

My advice? Stick to Scripture. If God says do it, then do it. If he says don't do it, then don't. Utilize another Christian's advice as a resource, but don't blindly adopt it as a lifestyle without careful thought and prayer. While much of his or her advice may be helpful and beneficial to follow, no human is infallible. God's Word is infallible, yes, but interpretations of it can vary or even seriously miss the mark.

Refuse to get tangled up in arguments about what your marriage must look like. Remember, we're talking dancing here. You and your husband may be doing the rumba. The couple across town is dancing the cha-cha, and Todd and I will be performing, of course, the fox-trot. But common to all well-executed dances is this: *let the guy lead.*

For the love of Fred and Ginger, just how do we do that?

Here are five key dance steps to follow:

1. Realize that the act of submitting is always a choice by and an action of the wife.

The Bible doesn't say, "Husbands, see to it that your wife submits to you." No way. If you think submission allows the husband to be a male chauvinist and demand that his wife do whatever he says no matter how unreasonable it is, then you, my dear, have been given an incorrect and corrupt picture.

The wife is told she should adapt. She can decide whether to obey Scripture or not. Never is the husband told to "make her behave." He has his own set of instructions, which are to love, to be affectionate and sympathetic, to not be harsh, bitter, or resentful. And hey, who wouldn't want to adapt herself to a man who treated a woman like that? Willingly adapting is your business, not the hubster's.

2. Know that backing off and not controlling your husband will feel very foreign.

If God knew it would be easy for us to stop controlling our husbands, he wouldn't have included verses and instructions to us about doing so. Again, controlling things is a strength carried to an extreme that becomes a weakness. Sure, women are skilled at making decisions. But God wants us to make them in tandem with our husbands. Cooperation is lovely. Overcontrol is ugly.

Of course we can voice our opinions. We should be our husbands' first and greatest advisers. Especially when it comes to the children. Women have many keen insights, intuitions, and ideas on so many fronts. A man who doesn't look to his wife for advice, counsel, and input is, in my estimation, shooting himself in the foot. And it's kind of hard to do the *paso doble* with a bullet-ridden foot!

Just remember that attempting to hold our tongues, let our men lead, and not criticize or complain will take discipline and effort. But the results are worth the strain. As the author of Hebrews wrote, "No discipline seems enjoyable at the time, but painful. Later on, however, it yields the fruit of peace and righteousness to those who have been trained by it" (12:11 HCSB).

Acquiring the discipline of letting go and not being a control freak with my husband is certainly no picnic. It's painful. But peace and righteousness are fruits I consistently want to grow in my life. So if I can get them only by the training that results from focused and sometimes painful discipline, then I say let the workouts begin!

3. Next, recognize the subtle difference between manipulation and influence.

My friend Dr. Juli Slattery of Focus on the Family, in her practical and biblical marriage book *Finding the Hero in Your Husband*, wrote this:

> Once when I was speaking to a group of women, one of them asked me, "What is the difference between manipulation and influence?" What a great question! Wives are called to use their influence to help their husbands — not to manipulate. The spirit of influence is to *help* him make a good decision based on giving him additional information. The motive of manipulating is to limit a person's choice by "stacking the deck" unfairly. Influence is overt and clear. However, manipulation can be subtle and deceptive.[2]

What relevant advice! When we twist what could be God-glorifying influence and morph it into manipulation, we cross the line, and the results are not good. Oh, we may get our way, but we'll be going against the directives of Scripture to do so. And if our chief aim is to glorify God, we've missed the mark by a long shot. Influence your man, but stop short of all-out manipulation.

4. Then find the unique dance steps that work for your marriage.

I don't know how others do it, but somehow they can study the same Bible I have and then promptly put in place rules and roles that I never seem to spot. Such as it's only the man's job to ever touch the checkbook.

Now I have a loyal but also very opinionated and vocal friend. She learned once upon a time, from someone whose spiritual advice she follows to the letter, that it's only the husband's job to manage the checkbook and none of the wife's business. So she never writes a check. Her husband gives her money for the weekly groceries. She asks him for money for purchases she'd like to make.

I have no trouble whatsoever with their financial arrangement. It works for them. What I have trouble with is the way she made many young brides and fellow church wives feel like they were in error if they too didn't adopt said payment plan.

One wife did. She grew so "convicted" (and wanted so to be liked by the vocal wife) that she marched home and told her husband she repented of handling the family money (by keeping and balancing the checkbook). Since he was the head of the home, it was his job to keep the ledger from now on. She was through. She handed the financial reins over to her bewildered hubby.

On the surface she seemed to relinquish control. In reality she was allowing herself to be controlled by her friend's opinion and then in turn was controlling her husband. There was no constructive discussion of the family checkbook logistics. She just put her foot down and demanded, "Here. You do this!"

Well, after three weeks and about four bounced checks, her frustrated life partner came to her and announced, "You know, you're right about something. I am the head of this house, so I'm ordering *you* to keep the checkbook!"

He hated balancing the checkbook. It just wasn't his thing. It took time away from other tasks at home and at work. It completely frustrated him, and besides, he asserted, no real decision making was going on here. In their original setup, the wife never made a major purchase without running it by her husband. If a check needed to be written to the power company for ninety-eight dollars, then someone just needed to write the check (or pay it online), and most importantly, do it *before* the due date, which he just couldn't seem to swing with his demanding work schedule.

Their original groove was working just fine. They'd divvied up responsibilities based on interest, availability, and skill. The wife had all of these when it came to being keeper of the checkbook.

They had a good chuckle (well, after they paid all the overdraft fees) and returned to their initial setup.

As you and your husband communicate, ponder, and pray about this, you'll ascertain the cadence that works for your marriage. Yes, you as a wife will advise and influence, but you'll follow his lead. Your dance may travel to your side at times before shifting directions his way for a while. Other times you may stay stuck in a spin till your head becomes dizzy. Eventually you'll find a distinctive "ours" — the rhythm that works for you both.

It's all good. If it's all God. Not just Brother So-and-So's predrawn blueprint.

God wants you and your spouse to hammer out the particulars that make your marriage a uniquely "ours" display of glory. Through the process of prayer and communication, you and your husband will bond, and the bond will be strong. It's easier to simply follow another's blueprint of conviction than it is to craft your own. But the results aren't nearly as gratifying.

5. Recognize when you need dancing lessons from a pro.

Sometimes, no matter how much you try, you and your partner keep stumbling over each other's feet. Or your husband utterly refuses to dance. Or worse yet, he stomps on your feet. What then?

All marriages have strife. Personality quirks that cause clashes or male-female differences that frustrate and cause friction are completely normal. These little missteps require adjustment and grace, give and take. Some situations, however, aren't so easy to work through. At times you may need to take a few lessons from a pro, someone trained in biblical counseling who can keep you and your spouse from tripping over each other's feet and making a mighty mess of the entire marriage dance.

Scripture is clear that there is wisdom in consulting godly counselors and mentors, and indeed, you and your husband may readily seek counsel when it comes to your parenting or your walks with Christ. When it comes to marriage, however, sometimes you may balk. You may think that admitting you need outside counsel says you're weak. Or that you're a failure. Nothing could be further from the truth! Seeking help to push through a rough spot in your marriage is courageous and wise. It can strengthen your commitment and better your entire family. Take advantage of those who have expertise in the area of godly marriage.

Finally, if your situation is more than just a little rough and instead is quite serious, know when to take drastic action. I have walked through some challenging marital times with close friends and extended-family members. Some of the issues these women faced included emotional abuse, alcoholism, destructive addictions, and even physical harm. In such serious cases as these, professional help is almost always needed. A wife might need to exercise some control over the situation by removing herself, and perhaps her children, from harm's way.

If you're in such a hard place, please seek help. Pray for God's perspective and clear direction as to the steps you must take. It takes two people to make a great marriage. Unfortunately, it takes only one person to break up a marriage. If your husband decides he no longer wants to dance, or if he is moving in a way that is dangerous, get help and get out if you must.

Made in Heaven; Performed on Earth

It's been more than twenty-five years since I first laid eyes on foxy Todd Ehman. His auburn hair is no more, taken by a harmless bout of alopecia five years ago. His eyes still remind me of the glassy, green sea. But when I look at him now, I see not necessarily a young, chiseled body but a chisel instead.

God has used our marriage as a tool to chip away at my pride, to whittle away the parts of me that think (or sometimes know!) I'm always right. As God strives to make me more like his Son, he sees the parts of me that must fade away.

Women sometimes ask if I ever wish Todd and I had a breezier and easier marriage, since our marriage hasn't always been the proverbial walk in the park.

I can honestly answer, "No." And you want to know why?

Because my marriage keeps me on my knees.

You see, if I had a perfect husband who could meet my every need, I would have no need for God.

And if he had a flawless wife who never yelled or nagged or

overcontrolled (not that I ever do those things!), he might not think he had need for a Savior. As my friend Lysa TerKeurst told me once, "Even a really great spouse makes a very poor God."

So that's why I'm thankful I have a husband who drives me nuts (and he, a wife who drives him even nuttier!).

Because . . . it drives us both straight to Jesus.

And if this whole marriage-dance thing came easy, I wouldn't experience the joy of being trained for peace and righteousness as I learn to stop trying to control my husband and let him lead. Or discover the thrill of letting go and trusting God, not Todd (which is really at the heart of the matter, ladies).

Do we really trust God? Do we take him at his word? If he says we're to adapt and adjust while our husbands love and lead, do we somehow think he meant that for every other duo, but somehow our marriage is the exception?

Well, are you up for a challenge?

If so, I double dare you to . . .

decide to stop deciding all the time.

step back at times so he can step up.

let go sometimes so he can take charge.

influence but don't manipulate.

stop managing your man and start trusting God.

discover the amazing superhero you have in your very simple husband.

experience the thrill of the glorifying dance, as together you and your own handsome hubby pronounce to each other, as the Master Conductor strikes up the band, "Listen, honey, he's playing our song!"

Getting in the Groove with Your Groom

Rate the following areas of your marriage on a scale of 1–5, using this key:

1. extremely passive and compliant
2. somewhat passive
3. average
4. somewhat controlling
5. overly opinionated and controlling

Use a pencil to circle the number that best represents how controlling you are about the subject listed. Then mark a square around the number that best indicates how controlling your husband is about that matter.

Okay, have at it!

Spending money

1   2   3   4   5

The cleanliness of the house

1   2   3   4   5

The condition of vehicle exteriors and interiors

1   2   3   4   5

The arrangement of your garage

1   2   3   4   5

The yard's appearance

1   2   3   4   5

The arrangement and cleanliness of the fridge

1   (2)   3   4   5

The paper piles in the home

1   2   [3]   4   5

The kids' chores

1   (2)   3   4   5

The weekends' agendas

1   2   [3]   4   5

The kids' bedtime routine

1   2   3   [4]   5

Vacation plans

1   [2]   3   (4)   5

The frequency of one-on-one communication between you two

1   [2]   3   4   5

Holiday plans

1   (2)   3   4   5

The kids' homework getting done

1   2   3   (4)   5

The frequency of "horizontal fellowship" (the code term Todd and I have for intimacy ☺)

(1)   2   [3]   4   5

Next, use this section to dialogue with your man about how you can best find your unique groove. Read aloud the listed areas one by one. Ask him how he would rate himself and what ranking he would give to you. Do your answers match?

Without fighting, pouting, or finger pointing (I know, that's a tall order to fill!), discuss what your method for dealing with each area of your marriage will be. Are there ground rules you can lay? Rules of thumb by which you can operate? Steps you can take when the topic comes up to ensure you're both in sync?

For example: In the area of spending money, let's say you're a 5 (very controlling about it) and your hubby is a 2 (somewhat passive about it). You might establish the following guidelines:

Spouse A will pay the monthly bills.

Spouse B will balance the checkbook, reconciling it with the bank's monthly statement. (It might be good to have both spouses' eyes on the checkbook, doing different jobs so each can get a handle on what's happening with the finances.)

No one spends more than twenty-five dollars on a single item without running it by the other person.

You — the more controlling one — will agree to seek your husband's opinion about optional (nonbill) spending and not just make purchases (or *refuse* to make purchases) all by yourself.

Together, you'll set a target budget for various categories. Perhaps an envelope with fifty dollars of "date money" a month for you two to eat out or go to the movies with, or one hundred dollars of "fun money" a month so the family can do an activity together.

Are there even more areas you can think of that need to be discussed? Set a time now to go over this exercise with your husband to discover the particular "dance" that is yours.

CHAPTER 5

Micromanaging Instead of Mothering

Sweater — n.: a garment worn by child when its mother is feeling chilly.
Ambrose Bierce, American journalist, 1842 – 1913

When you are a mother, you are never really alone in your thoughts. A mother always has to think twice, once for herself and once for her child.
Sophia Loren

But we behaved gently when we were among you, like a devoted mother nursing and cherishing her own children. So, being thus tenderly and affectionately desirous of you, we continued to share with you not only God's good news (the Gospel) but also our own lives as well, for you had become so very dear to us.
1 Thessalonians 2:7 – 8 (AMP)

I don't believe any woman sets out to be a bad mom. She doesn't dream of her parenting style securing a featured spot someday on national TV, perched on Dr. Psychologist's "Monster Mom" couch, the spot reserved front and center of the watching world for the mothers who messed up their kids.

Even so, my out-of-the-chutes mothering was a catastrophe. Caring for a little person round the clock cramped my independent style. I couldn't come and go as I pleased. Or take a break for very long. Just as soon as I did, baby Mackenzie might need to eat. And though she had a fabulous, hands-on daddy who could hold her when she cried and change a diaper with the best of them, he simply didn't have the goods to make her hunger go away.

For months I felt controlled by my child. When she whimpered, I picked her up. When she was hungry, I nursed and burped her. And even when she was awake, I felt I needed to hold her (because of something someone told me about Einstein attributing his intelligence to the fact that his feet rarely touched the ground until he was near the age of three). I really thought I was taking my plays right out of *The Good Mom's Handbook*.

But about the time she turned one, I'd had enough. Being at her beck and call was exhausting. She still hadn't slept through the night — and wouldn't until nearly the age of three! Finally I decided that this minuscule tyrant in her pink-footed jammies was *not* going to call the shots anymore.

Enter Micromanaging Mom! (Make my cape turquoise, please. It's my very best color.)

The dictionary defines a *micromanager* as "someone who wants to control every part of a business or system in a way that is not necessary or useful."

I don't know how I crossed over from being a pushover to being a micromanager of my children, getting all up in their business, but I did. And I hate to admit it, but at the heart of the switch again was control.

Parenting for Appearances

Early in my parenting adventure, I was beginning to pick up on subtle hints (from my friends) and not-so-subtle hints (from the in-laws and outlaws) that I was letting this pint-sized princess rule the roost, and it had better stop before she transformed from Snow White into the Wicked Queen. I wanted to control what they thought of me as a mom, so I vowed that things around our abode would change and change fast.

And so it began. I read every parenting book I could get my hands on. (You know the kind: *12 Simple Steps to Making Your Child Obey Perfectly* or *Authoritative Mothering* or *Pushy Parenting 101.)* These books were supposed to tell me how to get my child's behavior under my control. But I didn't stop there. I also sought out advice, both in person and in print, on how to crank out kids whose character was impeccable.

I reasoned that if I followed all of the 1-2-3 steps and applied the slick spiritual principles to an ever-lovin' *T* (for training), the result would be a perfectly compliant creature. This would promptly elect me Most Effective Mom of the Year in my circle of peeps. The only trouble was, I cared much more for what my peeps and relations thought of my mothering prowess than about how it would affect my relationship with my child.

Whipped into Shape?

I know kids need boundaries and fences. They need to know the rules of the house (and the whys behind the rules) and the expectations from the parents in charge. Most of all, they need to be taught from the time they are ankle-biting babes that there is a God who created them and who knows best how they should live their young lives.

In training a child (of which I don't claim to be an expert, by the way. One has now flown successfully from our coop. The jury is still out on numbers two and three), I learned very quickly that I needed to have a parenting plumb line, a point of reference from which my husband and I would make rules and set boundaries. I also needed to have an end goal in mind.

As the old saying goes, "If you aim for nothing, you'll hit it every time."

But because I so wanted *others* to see my children behave, I sometimes set unrealistic expectations for my offspring. I expected them to behave in a manner far beyond their years. Or I didn't teach and train them, allowing for mistakes and missteps that would be corrected along the journey. I told and scolded, maneuvered and manipulated, and grew my kiddos nice little ulcers.

I also felt as though I was being compared to the other mothers in my life, the church ladies whose offspring never seemed to misbehave when we visited after the service on Sunday morning. Even as preschoolers and elementary-age youth, their children uttered "yes, ma'am" and "no, sir" on cue. They stood at attention when adults were speaking, and they minded their parents — get this — *the first time they were asked.*

My sweet and adventurous daughter, by contrast, was scaling the kneeling prayer rails as her own personal jungle gym, wouldn't come the first time I called, and hollered, "Watch it, lady!" when she passed a senior saint in the hall carrying a casserole to the church potluck. Mercy! And her daddy was the church's youth pastor. I knew we were being watched with an even closer eye than other young parents in the pews.

And so, wanting to know their secret to behavioral success, I asked. Many recommended a particular book that was popular at the time. Suffice it to say, it touted not only a heavy hand of control but also a tool of correction that would *literally* whip the rambunctious rowdies into shape in no time.

Yes, I said *whip.*

I started reading the first few chapters. Thankfully (and also tragically — you'll see), God orchestrated an outing soon after I began reading that book that gave me a real-time snapshot of this method of child training.

A new friend, who was raising her nearly half-dozen sweet darlings by said handbook, and I decided to go out garage saling together on a spring Saturday morning.

My friend's shy, four-year-old daughter was assigned a seat between her mom and me — her mom was driving, and my bargain-hunting fanny was parked in the front passenger seat. (This was before the many warnings about having a child in the front seat of a vehicle.) But this precious girl didn't want to sit there. She wanted to sit in the back with her siblings.

She asked her mother kindly if she could sit in the back. Her mom's immediate and rigid response was "Absolutely not. I told you to sit here, so do it now or you'll get 'the rod.'" This mom believed in wielding absolute control over a child's behavior.

Now in the little girl's defense, I don't think her intent was to disobey her mom. She was usually sweetly compliant. I think, instead, she was frightened. She didn't know me at all. I could tell from the look on her face and the timid glance of her eyes that she felt much more at home nestled among her brothers and sisters than tucked in between Momma and her new, unfamiliar friend.

"Why don't we switch her with the baby?" I offered, trying to defuse the situation that was about to ensue. My friend wouldn't hear of it. Her child had been told what to do, and my friend expected nothing less than complete and instant obedience.

When her daughter began to whimper, her mom whipped "it" out of her purse — her weapon of compliance she never left home without. Soon she began, right in front of me, to strike the top of her child's thighs until they were covered in red marks and starting to welt. Then she left the girl tightly buckled in the seat, sobbing silently into her mom's side.

I'd never felt so sick in all my life.

Later when I dared bring up the conflict, wanting to know how the precious girl's legs were feeling, her mom brushed it off, saying, "Her legs? Oh, that's nothing! Sally So-and-So whips her strongest-willed son's bottom until it looks like hamburger meat."

I never read the rest of the book.

Now nearly twenty years later, I've had the chance to interact with some young adults who were brought up by this method of overcontrolling child rearing. Some, by God's grace, have suffered no lasting effects. Others have a strained relationship with their parents and say that even from a tender age, they felt their parents cared more about impressing their friends with strict, ironfisted ways that produced seemingly perfect and obedient children than they did about what was going on in the heart and mind of their child.

A great number even jumped off the deep end spiritually as soon as they got out of the house, some landing in jail or strung out on drugs. They equated God with their parents. They surmised that he also must be harsh and unloving, so they wanted nothing to do with him or his people.

What's the Point?

Please don't misread my aversion to the aforementioned method of controlling your kids' behavior as a blanket statement on spanking. I am not antispanking. I am pro-God and pro-Bible. What I'm saying is that when it comes to the bazillions of parenting experts and advice out there, chew the Braeburn apple (my favorite) down to the core, but please make an effort to spit out the seeds.

Take advice prayerfully and carefully. Don't always buy into every lick of Mr. or Mrs. Parenting Expert's techniques without taking them before the Lord, holding them up to the light of Scripture, and hearing from God as to whether he'd recommend this particular method for that particular child.

Not every correction or penalty works with every single one of your dear dependents. The hubster and I learned this early on.

Take the consequences approach to discipline. Sometimes when our kids acted up or deliberately disobeyed, we'd make them head out into the heat and uproot some unwanted foliage in Mom's lovely and fragrant herb and perennial garden.

Our daughter hated this. She didn't like getting her hands dirty or chipping her sparkle nail polish. She hated to sweat. This consequence worked well for her. "Knock it off or you're gonna spend some quality time with some stubborn weeds" was often enough to get her to reconsider her actions.

But it didn't serve the same purpose with our oldest son, who got the combined genes of all four of his hardworking grandparents. When we sent him out back to pull the weeds, we didn't hear from him for the longest time. That was because he would pull the ones in the front yard too, even though it wasn't part of the punishment package. He'd come into the house sweaty and dirty and say, "Ya need any other yard work done?" (Of course he'd be expecting payment for any additional chores beyond what was initially assigned.)

For that child, whom we used to refer to as Mr. Big Bucks, we found that fining him an amount of money worked so much better. He loved his cashola, and knowing he might have to part with some of it — especially the folding green stuff he earned when he worked in Papa Pat's yard — well, it snapped him suddenly to attention.

Different strokes for different folks. And also for different siblings.

But with any correction, I have to ask myself, "What is the point?"

Am I trying to nip a destructive pattern or behavior?

Good.

Am I attempting to teach my children to respect the authority in their lives, which for now is their parents, so that one day they will respect their boss or the government or the police officer?

Excellent.

Am I trying to teach them diligence, patience, the value of hard work or honesty?

Wonderful.

But I also have to ask myself this: "Is this really a neutral issue, and I'm just trying to control my child and get my own way? Am I hurting my child (physically or emotionally) because of my own needs?"

Bingo!

We control-freak-leaning mommas do this all the time.

Turning into a Tin-Pot Dictator

Let's say the dishes need to be done. The dishwasher is on the blink. If Micromanaging Momma were to do them, she'd do them in the proper order, the logical sequence she learned in home ec.

Glasses first. (They are the least soiled.) Then silverware. Next, plates and bowls. Finally the crusted-on prep pans and baking dishes, which may need to soak awhile. Because Mom would work from least to most dirty, she wouldn't need to change the water as often.

I'll bet she'd even have a chosen method for stacking the dishes to dry. (You should see my husband's towers. They are tall works of art and don't topple over like they would if I attempted to erect one. Yes, I love me a man with dishpan hands!)

Well, instead, Junior is going to do the dishes today as part of his chores. A smart preteen, he is certainly up to the challenge. So why does it threaten to turn Mom into a tin-pot dictator, throwing her weight around in her own personal banana republic?

Because Junior failed to do the dishes her way.

He started with the grimy pots and pans because he likes to get them out of the way. Next, he moved to the plates and bowls, tossing in the silverware to make things move faster. Finally, he had to bubble up more water to spit-shine the glasses and stemware before calling it a day. During the execution, he lollygagged and dawdled, trying to stack some plastic cups in a pyramid in between rounds. He also spread out twice the amount of towels Mom would have used to house the overflow of dishes, allowing them to dry.

What most likely will happen if Mom reacts to Junior's unconventional way of washing dishes without asking the Holy Spirit to temper her response?

We already called it — she'll turn into Kim Jong-Ugh. Let's pick up Micromanaging Momma and her running and cutting commentary.

"What are you doing? Don't you know it uses way more water to wash the dishes in that order?"

"Stop playing stack-up with those cups. They're going to fall! Ugh! Why do you always have to play while you work? You are so inefficient."

"Aren't you done yet? You are so slow."

What is really going on here? Momma is turning into a tin-pot dictator.

She thinks the only way to do the dishes is her way.

She thinks everyone else should also do them her way.

She sees different as wrong.

Saving water (and money on water and dish soap) is important to her.

She interprets a preteen being a preteen, with a slight distraction of fun, as "slow."

She probably has pent-up anger and frustration over the dishwasher being busted in the first place.

Oh, and she unloads it all on Junior, who is only acting his age and accomplishing a task he was assigned in the way that currently makes the most sense to him and fits with his personality makeup and age. The result of Mom's response is that their relationship is damaged and seeds are planted in Junior's mind of his mom's view of him — whether that view was actually verbalized or merely implied (lazy, wasteful, distracted, and slow).

This doesn't make for a happy home.

The scenario could have gone down so much differently.

Let's back up the minivan and try this again, this time with a fresh dose of perspective and a God-glorifying and Spirit-controlled response.

Mom spies Junior doing the dishes in his own unique way and holds her tongue. (Bite down if you must. Better a mom's bleeding tongue than a son's battered heart.)

As she sees Junior do the dishes in his illogical order, she can make a mental note to herself to explain to Junior, the next time she does the dishes, the way to do it that will save water, money, and perhaps even some of Junior's time. Of course, there are times she could sweetly point out tips immediately.

When he's done, she can praise Junior's efforts, no matter how small, keeping in mind his age and abilities.

She can intentionally point out particulars in his personality or method — "I saw you stacking those dishes. You always have a way of making work fun. I wish I were more like you."

Moms with special-needs children, whether the issue is physical, emotional, or developmental, have a tougher road to trudge. Some of the "normal" expectations society and school have for children may be unattainable in the life of their son or daughter.

I have several friends and a cousin who parent children with either autism or Down syndrome. I marvel when I witness these friends' patience and perseverance. I cheer when I see their offspring take even the smallest social or academic steps. Often, when I compliment them on their prowess at parenting children who demand such individual and focused attention, I'm clued in to the fact that for them mothering is a moment-by-moment decision to depend on the Lord for strength, direction, and calm. They know they cannot be in control of their child's behavior at all times. They can serve as wonderful role models to the rest of us.

Todd and I don't have a child with physical special needs, but we do have a son who, like his father and an uncle, struggles with severe dyslexia. Sadly, when Mitchell was in grade school, I let his condition rob me of much joy. While other kids were devouring entire chapter books in an afternoon or two, Mitchell was still wrestling with two-syllable words. I fretted and cried and felt "left out" as a homeschool parent. I didn't give much thought to how Mitch might be feeling whenever he had to read aloud in Sunday school or at his educational co-op.

A decade after his diagnosis, I've purposed to cheer for even the small steps he makes in his academic progress without comparing him to my friends' kids who are making the honor role, taking advanced-placement classes, or becoming National Merit Scholars. I've learned that it's more important to recognize and praise effort and diligence than outcome and performance.

The task may be small, such as doing the dishes, or great, such as learning to read. Whatever the magnitude of the task, we moms would do well to examine our hearts. We can mentally ask ourselves questions that will empower us to maintain calm emotions and keep a healthy perspective. Questions like . . .

"Does it matter now?"

"Will it matter tomorrow?"

"Will it affect eternity?"

"Is God trying to teach *me* something? If so, what?"

"Can I pause and praise instead of interrupt and instigate?"

"Is there really an issue here that needs addressing with my child?"

"Am I just being a control freak, and do I need to let it go?"

In the earlier scenario, Micromanaging Momma can, the next time or even later in the evening, gently offer some suggestions to Junior. Of course, if it's a safety issue, like tossing sharp knives into murky water where they can cause injury, she should intervene immediately — but still gently.

If she takes the time to question herself, the interaction between Mom and Junior will be a learning experience for both. It won't damage. It will nurture. And there will be no lost time, no regrets, and no need to call in the UN peacekeeping forces for intervention.

Please know I am *not at all* polished when it comes to this process. I can describe it so well because I've had to make myself do it so often! My natural tendency would be to perform the script of the Micromanaging Momma we read about earlier.

Pampers: Not Just for Babies Anymore

The world certainly has its share of controlling parents. While some parents don't overcontrol their kids' behavior, they *do* overcontrol their experiences and opportunities. Yes, pampering wasn't just what Mrs. Oleson did to that brat Nellie in Walnut Grove (à la *Little House on the Prairie*). There are plenty of Nellies (and brother Willies) today too.

Pampering can come in the form of shielding our children from hurt. Never letting them experience wounded feelings or be left off the party invitation list or be excluded from the group of friends' activity. To ensure that no social sadness comes our child's way, we may pull strings, make calls, and give reasons why our darling should be included too.

Or it can show up by running interference for our children, wanting them to succeed in an ultracompetitive world. We may pave the way with lots of money, tutors, special training, or counseling. Or we may maneuver and manipulate to get our children into a certain school or to help them land a certain job. Some parents of adult children buy their kids cars, trips, or even homes. This pampering form of overcontrol is probably a flaw of affluent parents who have the financial means to create opportunities for their kids that they might not be able to earn on their own merit.

Jockeying for opportunities, perks, position, and accolades for our kids is control too. We might not be controlling their actions, but we're certainly trying to control circumstances so that our children get what they (or we) want.

If we're honest, we have to admit that we want to control many aspects of our children's existence, including their . . .

friends

schooling

academic progress

performance ability in sports, music, or other extracurricular endeavors

opportunities

clothing

music

screen time (movies, television, Internet, and video games)

speech (A *big* one for me. Being an author and speaker, I cringed when my child would declare, "Me an' Michael are going down to the creek." I'd say, "Who is 'mean Michael' and just who is your English teacher?" Unfortunately, for most of our school years, as a home-schooling family, the answer was "You are, Mom!")

spiritual lives

That last one's a biggie too.

We parents who are believers often try to control our children's spiritual lives. We may have a mental list of dos and don'ts that comprise a good Christian kid. You know, the actions the church folk will say make for a kiddo with a gleaming halo: do attend church twice on Sundays and midweek; do have personal devotions every day; do sit squirm-free during family devos. And the don'ts? Don't smoke or drink or chew, and don't go with guys who do (as an old high school chant used to say).

If we spy our kids not doing a "do" or toying with performing a "don't," we seek to correct their behavior. And pronto. While this may be a well-intentioned move, if not done with careful, prayerful love, it may only be outward correcting without a peek into the "why" of the action. Merely getting a child to jump through a spiritual hoop might keep up your reputation at church, but it may damage your relationship with your child. Proceed with addressing the issue, but address it in love. (That is, if there really is an issue. Does the Bible actually prescribe the magic number of times a week you should attend church?)

Allowing More Choices

Learning to transition from making all the choices for our kids when they are helpless infants to launching responsible and conscientious members of society eighteen short years later takes intentionality and effort. And a little thick skin.

When they are infants, we must feed, dress, bathe, and protect our helpless offspring. As they grow, they learn to do tasks for themselves. We discover they can pick out their own clothes. Put their own hair up in bows. Make a bed. Fold a towel.

We clap and cheer when they master such skills — *but wait* — and sometimes redo them right in front of their eyes. There is no quicker way to knock the wind out of our little life adventurers' sails than to resmooth their bedspreads after we've just given them an "Attaboy! Good job!"

Tell me, which speaks louder: the words or the redo?

As our children grow and mature, we must learn to let go,

allow them more choices (within boundaries), and let them fail. Yes, that's right. Years of parent watching has shown me that it's not a wise game plan to never allow any room in our child's life for failure. Some moms I know make every choice for their kids, won't allow them out of their sight, tell them how to dress and what music is godly or not, and handpick their every activity right up until they leave for college. (One woman even told me of a boy who, on the day he left for the university, asked his mom if he could have her permission to stop parting his hair and wear it spiked up instead!)

Yes, when they're toddlers and children, we must keep them from evil influences and surround them with good. But we can't possibly keep them in our sights round the clock until they move out of our homes. We have to model and teach and then eventually let them have a stab at making their own decisions.

We must empower our growing kids to make good choices.

Please reread that sentence. *They* need to make the choices. Not us. And for them to do so, we need to learn to slowly loosen our grip.

Sometimes we grip our kids too tightly in our clenched fist. We never loosen it even a little. It feels good to be in command.

Then, one day, when our kids are ready to go off on their own, we're forced to suddenly open our fist and expect them to fly. Because they've had no practice in deciding for themselves right from wrong or in learning the biblical process for making healthy choices, they dart off in one of two directions.

Finally able to take a deep breath, perhaps they decide that freedom is for them. No longer confined and smothered, they wonder just what Mom and Dad have been keeping them from all these years. So they dive headfirst into the world and its

99

ways. But they don't make good choices, because they've never learned how.

Or they flounder about, since they haven't learned how to think for themselves. The world of adulthood is enormous and engulfing. They're expected to behave and choose like adults, but emotionally they're still babes. So back to the nest, either emotionally, physically, or both, they swiftly fly. And there they stay for years.

Certainly there are times adult kids need some help. But constantly smoothing their way or making all your children's choices for them and never allowing them to choose wrongly and then suffer the consequences is no way to teach reasoning, responsibility, and reliance on God. Even the very best parent makes for a very poor God.

Turning Over the Reins

So how do you let go slowly and intentionally? Here are some tips I've picked up over the years for gradually turning the reins of decision making over to your child:

1. In the toddler years, offer your kids choices that don't really matter.

Must they don clothes that perfectly match? Does it matter that they wear stripes with plaid and that neither color scheme is remotely of the same palette? So what if your daughter's ponytail is crooked. (Unless, of course, you're attending a family wedding or such.) Allow your kids to get the feel for making a choice.

2. In the elementary years, teach your children boundaries and consequences, but also tell them *why*.

For example: You may play with Johnny or Levi or Annie or Mandie. We know their parents. We have similar rules at our houses as far as movies and TV and video games go. You may not, however, go inside the house of anyone else in the neighborhood unless you first check with us. We don't know what their rules are. They may allow activities we don't believe are good for you or would please God. So if we find out (and we will) that you disobey us, you won't play with any friends for the next week.

It's also helpful to tell a story that illustrates your point. Maybe about boundaries and injuries. (A great resource is *The Children's Book of Virtues* by William Bennett. We read our kids stories from this book and from the Bible to illustrate vividly a point we were trying to make.) Todd and I are firm believers that when it comes to kids, it's most effective to not just tell them but show them. And nothing "shows" better than a story, a video clip, or a real-life tale. Pray that God will bring them your way, and he will answer that prayer.

3. In middle school, allow your kids to set some of their own boundaries and the corresponding consequences for crossing the line.

Sit down with your children. Work through some expected behaviors, household responsibilities, and social guidelines. Also talk about what would be some reasonable yet effective deterrents to outright disobedience (when they do something they knew they were forbidden to do) or bad behavior (when they do something that, while not explicitly forbidden to do, was either sinful or stupid).

I'm sorry to inform you that at least sometime in their childhood, they will exhibit both outright disobedience and bad behavior. And if you get your children to adulthood and you think they've done neither of these things, what they *have* done is a brilliant job of covering it up!

When your kids have some say in the process, they feel a sense of ownership and will be more likely to toe the line and less likely to balk at the consequences, since they helped invent them.

Now this isn't "pick a punishment," which our middle schooler tries to play with us. When he's facing the loss of a privilege or a party (the best way to penalize Mr. Social), he'll say, "Take away the varsity football game, but please not Blake's party!" The clever kid sometimes even begs backward so we take away the one he asked to keep. Only afterward do we find out the one we took away was actually the one he didn't care two hoots about.

Rather, this method of involving your children in setting boundaries and consequences is an attempt to indoctrinate them into life in general. Society has laws and rules. Bad behavior has consequences. Breaking the law brings a fine or sentence. Through our democratic form of government, we have a say in what laws will be enacted by being able to elect our representatives. So on a microcosmic level, you're inviting your children to discover how this works.

4. In high school, treat your kids like young adults, not babies.

Oh, this is so hard! When your fist is almost unclenched and your baby birds are test-driving their frail, underdeveloped wings, it will tear your heart right in two, and it will toy with your emotions daily.

One day they'll make a wise choice. Yay!

The next they'll get in touch with their inner idiot, and you'll wonder, *What were they thinking?* The trouble is, they weren't.

Those who study the development of the brain say that the prefrontal cortex, the part of the brain that controls sound judgment and reasoning, isn't fully developed until a person reaches the age of twenty-five. This explains teens' sometimes back-and-forth behavior.

Still, fight the urge to step in and overcontrol. Help your children talk through options and possible scenarios. Enable them to think through matters to their logical ends. And then back off and let them decide. When they succeed, praise. When they fail, practice grace. (And yes, it takes practice.) Also fight the powerful urge to throw in an "I told you so."

Overall, don't beat yourself up over their bad choices. They aren't your fault. If you are to blame for their sin, then correspondingly you are also to take the credit for their righteous behavior. But your children are responsible for their actions, and God alone should be given credit for anything good and righteous in their conduct. Yes, equip them as best you can, but don't glean your identity from their decisions. It's God's job to be their God and your job to be their mom.

5. In college, remember that although your adult children will always be your children, they are now also full-fledged adults.

While this might seem obvious, you may need to remind yourself of it during this transitional phase. Others may look at your twenty-something offspring and see a young, independent man taking his place in society by attending college or trade school or becoming part of the workforce, but you may still see a little boy playing with trucks too near the road where he might get hurt!

You may want to intervene when you see your children making choices that will lead to heartache or trouble. You don't want to see them hurt or suffering from regret. However, sometimes you need to keep quiet and let them take a path that might temporarily sting but, in the end, will steer them in the direction of spiritual maturity and success in life.

Many colleges today complain about "hover mothers" or "helicopter parents" who have coddled and spoiled their children and can't seem to back off and let their children live their lives and make their own mistakes. Yes, some parents are too harsh. But many parents are too permissive. When a child becomes an adult, the permissive parent may overcontrol by contacting those who are now in authority over their child and requesting they be lenient with Junior as well. This hinders letting Junior really be an adult and instead keeps him tied to Mama's apron, not taking ownership of his decisions and the natural consequences.

Fight the urge to step in and intervene when God is trying to teach your adult children a life lesson. Do they know the difference between right and wrong? Have you given them the tools to make wise choices?

Okay, then. Back off. Hit your knees. Don't hit the phone. Know your role as a praying parent, not a meddling mother.

6. During all stages, point your children to your faith.

Naturally weave God, Jesus, the Holy Spirit, and the Bible into how your family does life. Not in a "God is gonna get you" sort of way. Or in a legalistic manner. And don't just *tell* your children that God is your plumb line for living life and that you long for every decision you make to glorify him. *Show* them by your attitudes and actions.

Season your instructions with grace.

Lace your decisions with Christ.

Make applying biblical principles around your home as natural as breathing.

Steer, cheer, and encourage instead of control.

Knit Scripture into your conversations, not as a weapon, but as a way of showing your children that God is right and good and knows what he's doing.

And don't forget to ask for forgiveness when you blow it.

As young people today grow up with turmoil and uncertainty in their world—both their personal world of coming of age and the world at large that often seems to be coming unglued—the last thing they need is a pestering parent, a meddlesome mom, or a control freak who wigs out about everything and anything and insists on only doing things her way.

What kids need is stability in their lives: a praying, involved mom who will guide and nurture them from the cradle to the graduation cap *without* micromanaging their every move.

What a thrill it will be to see your children finally take off the spiritual training wheels and try their own hand at riding life's two-wheeler alone. Of course you'll need to hold on and run beside them for a while, but the time will also come for you to let go and allow them to ride solo as they follow the King.

Remember, it's your job to teach your children to ride, not to pedal the bike for them.

Teach. Train. But know when it's time to let go and trust.

Oh, and you may want to have a stash of Band-Aids for that occasional spill and resulting skinned knee. No mom is ever beyond administering a little TLC to her kids, no matter their age.

Loosening the Reins

Let's take a little inventory of control tendencies in our mothering. Our desire to be conscientious and raise good, godly kids (a very worthy goal!) sometimes turns into an all-out control fest. Perhaps it's because we're controlling. But sometimes it's because *we're being controlled*. We then set out to make our kiddos behave to save our reputations as competent parents. We must continually ask ourselves, "Am I mothering or micromanaging?" Well, sister, grab a pencil and let's find out! Rate the following areas in your mothering on a scale of 1–5, using this key:

1. extremely passive and compliant
2. somewhat passive
3. average
4. somewhat controlling
5. overly opinionated and controlling

Use a pencil and circle the number that best represents how controlling you are about the subject listed. You might want to use different colors to represent each of your children.

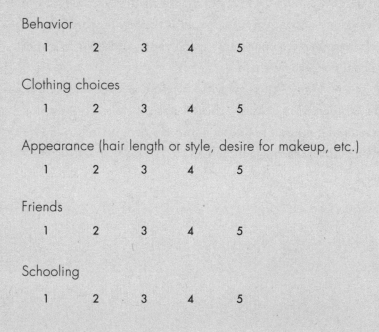

Behavior

    1   2   3   4   5

Clothing choices

    1   2   3   4   5

Appearance (hair length or style, desire for makeup, etc.)

    1   2   3   4   5

Friends

    1   2   3   4   5

Schooling

    1   2   3   4   5

Academic progress

    1   2   3   4   5

Performance in sports, music, or other extracurricular endeavors

    1   2   3   4   5

Opportunities

    1   2   3   4   5

Music choices

    1   2   3   4   5

Screen time (movies, television, Internet, and video games)

    1   2   3   4   5

Personal cleaning habits

    1   2   3   4   5

Interaction with grandparents

    1   2   3   4   5

Outward spiritual-life activities

    1   2   3   4   5

When you've identified areas of overcontrol, brainstorm ways you could turn over some control to your children, depending on their age and maturity level.

CHAPTER 6

Hovering Over the Home

Home is the place where we love best and grumble the most.
Billy Sunday

She watches over the activities of her household.
Proverbs 31:27 (HCSB)

As an eight-year-old, I couldn't think of anything more exciting than going to Sylvia's house for the afternoon. In a row of look-alike ranch-style homes, she lived in a two-story, the classy house with the long front porch and stately, white pillars that stood one street over in my mid-Michigan subdivision. Sylvia had fancy clothes and the neighborhood's only built-in swimming pool —*with* a diving board. But best of all?

Sylvia had one killer dollhouse.

This dollhouse wasn't just a plastic, store-bought contraption with a few basic pieces to complete it. No, sirree! This darling mansion was on serious doll-designer steroids! There were bedroom sets with dressers, cloth curtains in the windows, and colorful bedspreads on the beds. There was a living-room set with a teeny television and a kitchen with real-looking appliances in the ever-trendy shade of turquoise. It had minuscule dishes and rugs, candlesticks and clocks.

Yes, Sylvia's plaything earned a spot in *Better Homes and Gardens Dollhouse Edition.*

To top it all off, it came with a family —a tiny, pliable family full of lifelike, miniature human beings who smiled no matter how posed: Mom, Dad, three kids, a baby, and even a trusty canine I called Scrappy.

It was a miniature world of domestic bliss. *Sigh* . . .

I loved playing with Sylvia's dollhouse and accompanying family. I could arrange the furniture any way I desired. I'd park the petite little pots and pans on the stove while supper was simmering. I'd position Dad out in the backyard mowing the lawn while Scrappy played fetch with one of the children. The baby woke up from her nap just when I wanted her to. The family members entered and exited on my cue.

When I announced it was time to eat, all of the family members came scurrying to their assigned seats, smiles still plastered on their faces. They'd eat, and then it was back to their assigned imaginary roles. Not one inanimate object ever missed a single prompt in the scenario that played out at the end of my chubby little fingertips.

However, sometimes my mom — the mother who faintly smelled of Tabu perfume — would call me home for supper. When she called, I came running.

I'd hop on my purple Schwinn bicycle with the sparkly banana seat and pedal as fast as I could down Caldwell's hill and up the one in my own backyard.

Home.

I'd wolf down my dinner (Lipton Onion Soup Mix meat loaf, creamy scalloped potatoes, and the most colorful gelatin fruit salad, circa 1972, you'd ever seen). Then I'd give Mom a kiss on her cheek and hop back on my waiting bike to pedal back to Sylvia's.

If, by chance, one of the other girls from the neighborhood had happened by in the interim, longing to play with "the house," or if Sylvia herself wanted some time with her own toy, well, then my perfect little world was suddenly shattered, rearranged by someone who wasn't going along with my projected program.

I never liked when people messed with my plan, my scripted scenario of what life looked like within the dollhouse's four walls.

Well, the calendar on my wall no longer reads 1972. However, my days still revolve around a house. The furniture is bigger and much more expensive than the pieces inside little Sylvia's treasure. The dishes and rugs are real. The people are too.

And I still don't like anyone messing with my plans.

Homemaker Horrors

I've never fancied the word *housewife*. It sounds like a woman is married to her home. I much prefer homemaker, as in "I am trying to make a welcoming home for my family." Whatever term you use, you can bet your sweet potatoes that when it comes to the home, you're most likely the one who has high hopes of establishing order and calm and yet often can't seem to get your family on the same page.

You straighten and pick up, clean and spit-shine. You're intentional about getting all of your ducks in a row. And then? Along comes one of your own little ducklings knocking them down, forcing you to start all over again. Dad drops his socks on the bedroom floor — the floor you just picked up and then spent time vacuuming.

Or you may have used a little elbow grease to wipe down all of the kitchen counters and empty the dishwasher. No sooner have you moved on to another room than a child residing within your four walls decides to make a snack, leaving a trail of cheesy crumbs and soda drips on your newly shined surface and a dirty dish or two in his wake.

Or you leave a list of tasks to be done when you're away for the day. And an — *unspoken* — expectation of just how they are to be done. Or you post a list of foods to eat that aren't deemed off-limits. However, when you return home, the chores haven't been performed to your standards, and some foods you were planning on using later (like that shredded cheese for your Sunday casserole) are completely MIA!

It can make a woman blow a gasket. I know. After twenty-one years of parenting, I'm a top contender for Most Gaskets Blown in the mommy-meltdown category. (I'm sure many of you would argue that you'd take top prize.)

Well, instead of exchanging *Housewives Behaving Badly* horror stories about the times we allowed our tempers to get the best of us, let's talk solutions. What's realistic when addressing and assessing our homemaking routines? Should we lay down rules and processes in stone and expect that they be followed with precision? Or do we assume a laissez-faire attitude in which we don't force our poor brood to fuss with chores and chipping in around the ranch?

One extreme may appear harsh to our families, with no room for real life and even less room for grace. The other may find us wallowing in disorder, unable to function. And just how does allowing a free-for-all around the home teach kids responsibility, respect for another's property, and the value of hard work?

What is a homemaker — who wants to make a happy home — to do?

Let's start with a little mathematics lesson.

Two Plus Two Equals Four

My friend Rhonda told me about a method she uses when she is fretting and stewing because someone doesn't do things her way around the house. She said, "I just tell myself this: *Two plus two equals four. Three plus one equals four. Seven minus three equals four.*"

All her Jethro Bodine–like cipherin' lost me. So I asked her to please explain.

She clarified that she aims to remind herself often that there are many ways to get to the number four. Additionally (pun intended), there are many ways to accomplish tasks around the house, no matter who does them or how they get done.

For example, Rhonda might make lunch one way: microwaved leftovers, carrot sticks, and fruit. Her husband, when hanging out with the kids while Rhonda runs some errands, may tackle the job a completely different way: tuna-fish sandwiches, chips, and ice cream.

And her kiddos, when allowed to grab some lunch on their own, may go for a delightful buffet of frozen pizza rolls with a side of chips and cheese (nuked exactly twenty-eight seconds for optimum gooeyness, my boys tell me). And for dessert? Leftover Easter candy.

Bottom line? No matter what, lunch gets made. (Okay, okay, the kids' way isn't nutritious, but you must agree that they wouldn't go hungry.)

So why do we moms have to make a federal case out of a lunch crafted from items we personally wouldn't have served? Well, maybe you'd planned on using that ice cream for pie à la mode later at dinner. Okay. But did your hubby know that? If not, don't belittle the poor guy. Just go buy some more.

Does it *really* make a difference that lunch got on the table by a route you wouldn't have chosen?

Or let's talk laundry. As long as your family members don't mix colors, turning bright whites into pale pink, is it worth making a federal case out of their method of washing, drying, and putting away?

If you like to dust and then vacuum, but the hubby reverses the order, is it a hill you want to die on?

Remember, two plus two equals four. Three plus one equals four. It all equals four. (Rhonda tells me that during heightened moments of frustration, to keep herself calm she rattles off in her brain even more ways to four: *Thirty-six divided by nine equals four. The square root of sixteen is four!*)

Your turn. How many ways can you get to four?

Set the Tone

Now this little mental math lesson works much of the time, but we certainly can't just let things run amok in our homes while we meander about murmuring arithmetic equations to ourselves. A peek in Scripture shows us many places where we are to be proactive in not only setting the tone around our homes but intentionally making them run smoothly.

The oft-dreaded woman in Proverbs 31 (you know, the one the preacher drags out each Mother's Day as a shining example for all) was very proactive. (In the interest of saving space here, look up that chapter in a Bible or on a website such as *www .biblegateway.com*. Go ahead. I'll wait while you do.)

Back? Okay. Let's take a look at this popular homemaker of the Old Testament and the namesake of the Proverbs 31 Ministries for which I speak.

We see her rising before dark (verse 15), staying up late

(verse 18), and working with her hands (verses 13, 17, 19, and others). She was an on-purpose woman.

And, by the way, did you catch that it never stated she did all of those tasks in one single day? This chapter is a snapshot of her activities during her days (and years) of mothering and being a wife. So please take off the mental Superwoman cape you may have pinned on this biblical gal. She often gets a bum rap for being such a domestic diva, putting in eighteen-hour days and doing it with a smile. She actually was, in my mind, a regular mom who sought to serve an amazing God. His amazingness overshadowed her ordinariness, and that's what shines through.

She, like all of us, set the tone of the home. We moms set the mood and establish the atmosphere. Enough about the woman being inferior; she has enormous power! Unfortunately, like fire, when this power isn't used properly, instead of being helpful and life-giving, it can be detrimental and destructive. When we are overcontrolling and fail to apply any blessed control to our own tongues, domestic disaster may ensue.

I heard my friend Donna Otto (and a mentor mom to many through her books and speaking) say once, "Be a thermostat, not a thermometer. Set the tone and environment in your home."

But what kind of tone should we set?

Friendly, Not Feisty

"Okay, ladies," the guest speaker, my friend Sarah Eggerichs of Love and Respect Ministries, urged as she wrapped up her talk to my moms' group one night. "Now go home and be friendly in your homes."

Ouch! Had she *been* in my home just a few hours earlier?

Friendly was far from the way I had acted toward my brood. Unkind? Yes. Snippy? Certainly. Even caustic and cutting? Well, if I were honest, I'd have to declare a resounding *yes*.

Just what made this Jesus-professing mama behave in such an un-Christlike manner earlier that evening? Had someone acted rudely toward me? Had my kids disrespected me or my husband uttered something hurtful? Just what pushed my buttons and sent me over the edge?

Soiled socks. Smeared strawberry jam. Trailing crumbs. Dirty silverware and plates. And notebooks.

Oh, it wasn't just the presence of these items that sent ugly words soaring out of my mouth. It was the fact that just moments earlier, I had spent vast time and effort getting our great room spick-and-span clean. That meant a living area devoid of clutter, kitchen counters and tables wiped, all floors vacuumed, and surfaces dusted. I wanted the house tidied up so my husband and kids could relax while I was gone.

Then, in the short time it took to change clothes, spruce up my hair, add a dab of makeup, and grab my purse, my kiddos had, in my eyes, completely undone all my hard work! They'd whipped off their socks, made a snack of toasted homemade bread slathered with strawberry jam, and strewn their weekly Scripture memory books from a church program all over the place. It made my mama blood boil and resulted in feisty—not friendly—words.

I was working on a book on hospitality at the time and had been unpacking a key verse for my readers: "Above all, love each other deeply, because love covers over a multitude of sins. Offer hospitality to one another without grumbling" (1 Peter 4:8–9).

In the book I wanted to drive home the fact that hospitality—using our homes and lives as avenues of God's care for others — and love — the sacrificial placing of another human being above ourselves — are closely connected. And the most important element: we must both love and offer hospitality to others without grumbling. You know, be friendly!

Now, for the most part, aren't we able to do that when we have guests in our homes? We smile and serve and really don't get upset at crumbs and such. We happily wipe them up. Why is this so? And on a grander scale, why do we find it much easier to be friendly to complete strangers than to our own families? Do our tempers stay in check with the grocery-store cashier or even the dentist (whom I hate to see twice each year)?

Why is it so easy to snap at our kids, give our husbands the cold shoulder, or roll our eyes at a dear family member but remain gracious with those we meet in public, even when they do something that really grinds us?

I fear that many of us live out just such a contradiction in our daily lives. And what lasting pictures are our cherished children depositing into their memory banks? "Mom held it together when the dry cleaner completely ruined her favorite sweater, but she yelled at me for accidentally spilling grape juice on the carpet." Oh, sisters, this should not be!

Perhaps it's time to offer some friendliness to the members of our own homes, to keep our tempers in check and our grumbling at bay, to let perfect love wash over a multitude of sins. Not the jelly-smeared, crumb-laden kind, but the hideous-word-hurling, mama-mouthed variety.

Could we also let go of the deception of perfection, that desire to have the house looking magazine-perfect and every item in place? Here's a news flash for us half-happy homemakers: A tidy house is going to regularly untidy itself. The clean laundry will require washing again very, very soon. The belongings in our own larger-than-life dollhouses are going to get rearranged. Continually. When they do, are we going to badger and belittle or show grace and patience?

No doubt it's easy to be a control freak about the house. It's more difficult to apply a little control to our tempers and tongues. But when we do, we can set the tone in a way that invites Christ and calm into our homes rather than cutting words and chaos. Sometimes I wonder if I spent more time planning kind words than implementing around-the-house routines, perhaps my home would be more amiable.

Oh, may we Jesus-lovin' women choose to hesitate before we hurl. Rather than feisty, may we be friendly instead.

Wisdom and Faithful Instruction

But wait! The gal in Proverbs 31 had plans and routines. She didn't just sit back and let the home spiral out of control while she sweetly shrugged her shoulders, spoke kind words, and smiled acceptingly at the mounting mess. She was the picture of proactive productivity. And yet there is no mention of her doling out duties and then hollerin' at the hubby and kids when her plan wasn't followed precisely.

How did this industrious mom run her home efficiently and in a way that (as showcased in verse 26) her husband praised her and her kids called her awesome? (I know it says "blessed" in verse 28. I like *awesome*. The actual Hebrew word means "happy, fortunate, and to be envied." Sounds like *awesome* to me.)

Perhaps the praise from her husband and children had something to do with the statement in verse 26: "She speaks with wisdom, and faithful instruction is on her tongue." Can that be said of us? Or would a reporter standing by capturing (reality-TV style) the way we carry ourselves around the house

117

announce, "She snaps with caustic words, and 'Why can't yous' and 'You should haves' roll angrily off her tongue."

How can "wisdom and faithful instruction" keep things running smoothly around the house and relationships healthy and friendly?

I believe that all of Scripture is God-breathed (2 Timothy 3:16). I also don't think that the verses were just thrown together in a haphazard manner and then voilà!—here's the Bible. No, God chose each verse strategically and placed all of them in a purposeful and useful order.

That said, do you suppose it's a coincidence that verse 26—about speaking with wisdom and faithful instruction—comes just before verse 27, which declares, "She watches over the affairs of her household"? Nope. The two are closely connected.

It's our business as women to watch over the business of our homes. Though we shouldn't cut and control, posing our families like flexible figures in our own life-size dollhouses, we should be conscientious. This woman obviously was.

If we're supposed to watch over the affairs of our households—in other translations, "She looks well to how things go in her household" (AMP) and "She watches over the ways of her household" (NKJV)—then we must have some plans and routines in place (more on that at the end of the chapter). Often we become flustered with our families and want them to "get with the program!" while the crux of the quandary is that there is no program in place to get with except for the expectations in our own heads!

When giving instruction, it appears that this woman in the Hall of Fame of Scripture was careful to speak in a way that honored and glorified God. The Amplified Version, verse 26, rendered as close to the original language as possible, reads,

"She opens her mouth in skillful and godly Wisdom, and on her tongue is the law of kindness [giving counsel and instruction]."

Kindness.

The tone of voice you'd use with a stranger.

Friendly, not feisty.

And "giving counsel."

Counsel is giving advice and guidance in a gentle but direct way that helps the person seeking the instruction.

Counsel is not barking.

Counsel is not belittling.

Counsel is not filled with superlatives like "Why can't you ever ...?" and "See, you *never* ...!"

Yes, we should be conscientious, giving counsel; but we should not be controlling, or complaining with criticism.

House Rules in a Hushed Voice

On a particularly frustrating day that had my feathers ruffled and my emotions rattled, I happened upon Proverbs 15:1 — "A soft answer turns away wrath, / but a harsh word stirs up anger" (ESV). What a crucial verse for we women to memorize and seek to live out!

You know the scenario. You're trying to keep things hopping at your house. There are rooms that need to be picked up. Surfaces to clean. Foods to prepare. Tasks to be performed. Deadlines to meet.

All of a sudden, Junior wanders into your path with a question. You know, something life-shaking like "What's for dinner?" or "Why do I have to clean my room? Can't I go down to Zach's now to play?" It short-circuits your inner calm and pinches your very last frazzled nerve. Especially when dinner isn't for a couple hours, and the family is supposed to all be chipping in and cleaning their sections of the home, not dashing off to a friend's house. You surmise that you are busy doing your job around the home. Why doesn't the rest of the clan get crackin' and do the same?

How can you answer Junior's seemingly trivial question in a soft way, in a way that counsels and instructs? If you don't and instead let it set you off, the anger mentioned in the second half of that verse in Proverbs will ignite a firestorm.

I wish I could give you a magical answer. Some count-to-ten little chant or subconscious story line you could utter over and over in your sweet little brain that will keep your words and actions soft and not harsh.

However, twenty-five years of marriage and more than two decades of parenting have educated me to this fact: The fire doesn't ignite suddenly when the question is posed or the rule is broken or the household way isn't followed. Its kindling goes waaaaay back — back to expectations and perceptions. That's when the embers begin to glow and the fire's intensity starts to build. So we too have to back up — way back to the beginning — if we want to prevent a forest fire. (Smokey would be proud.)

We need to review the ground rules (or lack thereof) in our homes. We must determine whether they are unreasonable or fair. Does everyone understand them? Are any rules over the top and unnecessary, thereby showing our ugly roots of over-control? Are we enforcing the rules in an atmosphere of counsel and soft answers or in an environment of combat and criticism?

Here are some guidelines that have helped me find a measure of balance and establish some programs but also have grace with those in my home whom I expect to "get with the program."

Host a family summit.

Make sure that everyone, from parent to tot, understands that together, as a family, you are going to dialogue in a way that the various age groups present will understand the way the house is run.

Think through the various aspects of your home and try to gauge each person's expectations.

What do you and your spouse expect when it comes to the look of the house? Go through each room and try to verbalize what you as parents expect. Also take into consideration the thoughts and ideas of your kids. It helps to foster a feeling of belonging and ownership.

For example, take the mudroom, entryway, or kitchen—whichever room is directly inside the door your kids use when they return home from school or come in from playing outside with their friends. This room is usually the most disastrous. The kids drop what they're doing, literally, and it ends up a heaped-high mess of backpacks, jumbled shoes, wadded-up coats, and other assorted kid objects. (Open up that little hole in the top of your head now and cue the stack-blowing steam!)

Many heated words are exchanged over the condition of this room. But does it have to be this way? Strategize ways to remedy the problems of this room. Just make sure they're doable and not too complicated for the kids (or the parents!) in the family.

Perhaps the mudroom needs some hanging hooks installed for jackets. Maybe the kiddos have been dropping the jackets because the nearest coat closet is two rooms away. Hooks here will help.

How about getting some baskets, labeled with each child's name, that are cute and decorative? This way they can pull double

121

duty—both beauty and function. Train every child to place their items—backpacks, schoolbooks, and church papers—in the basket when they arrive home.

Recognize the trigger-point times.

Are there times during the week when you could bet your sweet bippy (don't ask me what that means; I just know my mom said it often) that conflict is sure to arise? Weekday mornings at 7:25 when you're trying to get the brood out the door and onto the bus? Sunday mornings at 9:15 when you're supposed to be on your way to worship but feel more like you're headed to war? Or the "arsenic hour," as my friend Susan refers to it—that period just before supper is to be served? (She named it such because during that hour you either want to take arsenic or administer it!)

Brainstorm ways to deflate the pressure and ward off the conflicts and spats. My friend Lori noticed that the first half hour after school when her kids arrived home was a prime time for routine and stupid fights between them. She sat them down and strategized ways to handle this. They decided on having a quiet time after school where they would each go to their own rooms or to separate parts of the house to chill out awhile. That greatly reduced the fighting.

Sometimes the strategy will be internal as well as external. For example, instead of fretting about your husband being on time for church, decide to let it go. Sometimes, drive a separate car so you and the kids who are ready will be on time. Don't get upset about being late. (Let the pastor chide from the pulpit; it's not your job.)

Pursue compromise.

While it may be your desire to have the place picked up and tidy, it may also be unreasonable to expect a hungry child, just through the door at the end of the day, to walk all the way up to her room and put all of her school belongings neatly away. A hefty yet attractive basket, positioned strategically only two or three steps into the entry point of the house, is a realistic and doable depository in the meantime.

Make a consequence, but also make it equitable.

Ponder the old punishment-must-fit-the-crime concept. Perhaps if your child doesn't place his items inside the basket in the entryway but rather scatters the items, drop-kick style, throughout the house, he won't be allowed any screen time (computer, television, or video games) until he migrates his items to the waiting basket.

Come up with some family sayings that will serve as a guide and ward off questions that may invoke a not-so-soft answer from you.

Like "work before play." With that phrase (that my kids could all parrot back by the age of four), you won't get as many "Can I go to so-and-so's house?" requests when there is work to be done. Your children will eventually (have patience) begin to self-police. They will recognize that if they want the privilege of play, they must first complete the duty of work. It's also a great motivating mantra for moms. I don't allow myself to open real mail, like cards and letters, or check out a new website I've been dying to see until my tasks at hand are complete. As a result, I work more efficiently and enjoy a fun reward when I'm done.

Praise often.

Why is it we parents are quick to correct our children when they are doing something wrong but are slow to applaud when they are acting as expected? Catch your children being conscientious. Did they place their school stuff in the designated area this afternoon without being told? Hunt them down. Give them a squeeze and say, "Thank you." Tell them you really appreciate them making an effort to do their part keeping things in place around the home. Are they attempting to follow the fridge and kitchen guidelines? Announce an impromptu trip to the ice-cream shop to reward them for doing their part in the operation of the home.

Embrace imperfect.

While making it a goal to have a place for everything and everything in its place, you must also get very acquainted with imperfect. And, more importantly, actually *delight* in imperfect.

Shoes strewn about means you have children who can walk. Mud-spattered uniforms means you have children who can run, jump, and kick. Homework papers left on the dining-room table means your kids have a functioning mind and are able to learn, absorb, and live quality lives.

Yes, have the expectations in place, but know that sometimes God wants you to whisper gratefully under your breath to him, aware that joy and thankfulness can be found in the imperfect parts of life and home.

Look for what God is doing in your heart.

If your existence as a woman consisted of a larger-than-life dollhouse with you in charge of your flex-and-pose posse, it might seem you'd finally be content. You'd be calling the shots, getting the results, and have no need for correcting your children in critical or combative ways. But you would also be missing out on important, faith-stretching sculpting God desires to do in your heart.

Learning to walk the fine line between being controlling and conscientious is a constant yet sanctifying struggle. It will keep you going to God for direction. It will find you asking for forgiveness for the times you blow it (there will be many). It will force you out of a stance of selfishness and into a posture of grace. You'll become skilled at putting others before yourself, adept at deference, familiar with compromise, and willing to yield your rights. You'll stop hovering over your home and start hallowing it—to *God's* glory, not your own. Yes, the process is hard. But the results are invaluable.

For me, though yielding doesn't come naturally, it stirs up an exhilarating feeling in my spirit that's even more thrilling than an eight-year-old playing with a real killer of a dollhouse.

A Domestic Diagnosis

Striking a balance in running a home is important. While we as moms shouldn't have to do it all, we also shouldn't just throw up our hands and let the appearance and function of our homes go completely out the window. (You know, that fingerprint-smudged window that hasn't been cleaned in months because no one has been assigned Windex duty!) Let's do a little diagnosis and intervention. Then we can come up with a fair and balanced plan for keeping things running smoothly and preventing us from running in circles while the rest of the fam lounges on the couch. Rate the following areas in your house on a scale of 1 – 3, using this key:

1. Nobody does much of anything, and it's a mess.
2. I have to do it all, and it drives me up a wall.
3. We each do our part to take responsibility for what is ours.

The mudroom or entryway

1   2   3

The bathroom(s) (identify problems with each, if you have more than one)

1   2   3

The kitchen

1   2   3

Food in the refrigerator and pantry

1   2   3

The family room

1   2   3

The bedrooms and/or office (identify problems with each)

1   2   3

The playroom

1   2   3

The garage

1   2   3

The storage room or basement

1   2   3

The yard

1   2   3

Unloading and putting away groceries

1   2   3

Lawn upkeep (mowing and weed pulling)

1   2   3

Weekly surface cleaning (dusting, vacuuming, scrubbing, etc.)

1   2   3

Bigger spring-cleaning chores

1   2   3

Paper issues (kids' school, church, and extracurricular papers)

1   2   3

When you've identified areas of neglect and/or conflict, host a family summit to strategize ways to tackle the problem areas.

Take a moment to identify the trigger-point places or times in your family life. How can you defuse those situations and help things run more smoothly? Are there areas of concern that exist because of lack of clarity regarding whose responsibilities they are? Remember, your clan can't "get with the program" if they don't know what the program is!

Hold a family meeting to discuss the current processes (or lack thereof). Brainstorm ways to divvy up chores and responsibilities so that everything doesn't fall on Mom's shoulders. Also decide what rewards and consequences will take place. Make sure everyone understands and agrees to whatever the family decides. A family contract might even be appropriate if you feel it would help. This works especially well if you have children who like to assert, "I never knew that!" when you know for certain that they did. Instead of arguing about what was said verbally, you can point them to the contract ... *ahem* ... that *they* signed!

CHAPTER 7

When Your Schedule Screams
(and You Want to Scream Too)

The future is something which everyone reaches at the rate of sixty
minutes an hour, whatever he does, whoever he is.
C. S. Lewis

There cannot be a crisis next week. My schedule is already full.
Henry A. Kissinger

But I trusted in, relied on, and was confident in You, O Lord; I
said, You are my God. My times are in Your hands.
Psalm 31:14–15 (AMP)

Suppose we were given the assignment of scripting out an
ordinary day, a blank twenty-four-hour time slot to fill any
way we choose, crafted to our liking, packed only with activities
we actually desire to do. How would you chart out the course for
your perfect, ordinary day? (No exotic getaways or over-the-top
dream vacations, now. We're talking a common day at home.)

Mine would begin with sleeping in. No alarms. No agenda.
No place to be by such-and-such a time. Oh, and no "Please
arrive fifteen minutes early to fill out the necessary paperwork." My perfect day wouldn't include a single stroke of
blasted paperwork.

Next, I'd partake of a healthy but delectable breakfast, fixed
by someone other than me, as my family and I shared laughs
and plans for the day. Once the clan was out the door, I'd enjoy

some time to sit alone and soak in a steaming froth of lavender-scented bubbles while I also soaked in the Word of God. (Yes, I am the giddy owner of one of those clever waterproof Bibles.)

Next, I'd head out for a leisurely stroll with a close friend or two through the local antique stores. Time-worn books with a vintage library aroma, delicate teacups for sipping afternoon tea, and retro holiday decorations needing a modern-day home would be the sought-after bargains on my list.

Afterward, Todd and I would meet for dinner at a bistro café, ending with fancy sweet coffee that would swirl beneath a whipped-cream cloud. I'd not once ever check my watch or cell phone for the current time.

In the evening, we'd all join back together as a family to watch a comedy as we lounged on our family-room sectional. And we'd end with a family talk-it-through Bible-study summit before heading off to bed, content and complete.

This setup would be a dreamy, relaxing experience I would gladly welcome any old day of the week!

What would be your perfect day? Just sit and fantasize for a few.

Got it all conjured up? Great.

Now let's snap ourselves back to reality.

Back to Life, Back to Reality

What is more true to script is the following scattered scenario.

You must be up early to start your day. And you must make sure all the little (and perhaps not-so-little) people are also up and at 'em. Either you are whisking folks — and perhaps yourself — out the door to school or an assigned occupation or hunkering down for a day of caring for others, working at home, or even a complicated combination of both.

Meals won't fix themselves. So you must plan, shop, put away, pull out, and prepare before anything even resembling a hearty meal or simple snack materializes on your table.

There are bills to pay. Kids to shuffle. Dry cleaning to retrieve. Bank deposits to be made. Emails to answer. Phone calls to make: "Please press one now. Now please hold for twenty-seven minutes until someone gets 'right with you,' since 'your call is important to us.'" Yeah, right . . .

The living room is in dire need of a deep carpet cleaning. So you must track down a reasonable and reputable business. Your in-laws need help. The dentist's office has a question about your insurance coverage and is expecting your call. But first you must call the insurance company. More holding and button pressing.

Your evening agenda boasts a church meeting, a run to the department store, and a walk of the family's trusty canine.

At the end of the day, you collapse into your still-unmade bed, only to set your alarm to "bright and early" so that tomorrow you can do it all over again.

Yep. Our schedule screams. As do our loved ones who need us to help them stick to their tight timetable too. And as much as we'd love to be in control of the clock, often it seems that our clocks, planners, calendars, and electronic gadgets (that house our appointments and beep warnings at us) are our time tyrants, running the hectic "keep running" show.

We try to squelch the screaming by being on top of things and in command. Because the schedule prods us to snap into action, into action we dive headlong. We grab the baton of control and keep things clipping along at breakneck speed, seldom slowing down. And all the while around us are living souls who, when they don't get with our program, immediately get on our nerves.

131

When an "Early" Marries a "Tardy"

Growing up, I learned the value of punctuality. My mom instilled it into us early. In fact, I can't ever remember being late to anything as long as I bore my maiden name.

For Mom, on time meant you arrived at least ten minutes early. Her first job as a preteen was in a canning factory. And now at nearly eighty years old, she still puts in a forty-hour week as an employee in a hospital's food-service department. Mom has never, *ever* been late to work a day in her life. (And she took only about a seven-year hiatus from work from the time she became a mom in the early 1960s until my brother and I entered grade school.)

Mom regularly builds extra time into her schedule. She arrives at work each day about forty-five minutes early to enjoy coffee with a girlfriend as well as to give herself a time buffer for traffic, crossing trains, and unforeseen delays. Why, once she even got a flat tire on the way to work. She had her car towed to a repair shop and then called for a cab and still clocked in a minute or two before her shift's starting time.

Marrying into my husband's family was, well, an adjustment when it came to time management and punctuality. Even in college, when Todd and I were dating, I heard a family friend of the Ehmans joke about "Todd Time."

"What is that?" I queried, eyebrows raised.

"Oh," she retorted, a smile on her lips. "Well, there's Eastern, Central, Mountain, and Pacific Standard Time, and then there's 'Todd Time.' Todd Time is fifteen minutes tardy to ordinary events and at least an hour late to bigger functions."

I was glad for the heads-up. It came in handy later when Todd and I were engaged. I purposefully misspoke and told my time-challenged fiancé that our nuptials were at noon, not 2:00

p.m., so as not to appear to be stranded at the altar. Can't you just see me turning to the crowd, trying not to ruffle my cathedral-length train? "Really, folks. It's okay. He's just on 'Todd Time.' Just talk among yourselves till he arrives."

I try not to fault the guy. He comes by this habit genetically.

When we were invited to our first Ehman family Thanksgiving gathering shortly after being married, I was told that dinner would be at 6:00 p.m. So I made sure my family genes trumped the hubster's that day so as not to arrive fashionably (and in my book, annoyingly) late.

We made the hour commute to his parents' homestead, arriving at 5:00 p.m. with our assigned dessert in tow. Plenty of time to visit with the in-laws before enjoying his mom's magnificent home cooking.

Well, the rest of the family finally sauntered in a tad before 7:00 p.m., with hugs and "how are yous" and "my, how you've growns," no one ever glancing at the clock or acting bothered by the lateness, both of which I was doing.

They started putzing around in the kitchen, peeling and plating, and finally broke out the to-die-for appetizers about thirty minutes later. The actual sitting-down dinner part began around eight o'clock, a full two hours behind the aforementioned schedule, irritating me to no end.

Suffice it to say, over the years I've had to learn to roll with it and realize this is just how things function in his family. (And Todd has had to put up with my get-there-super-early-just-to-be-safe philosophy, which drives him equally bonkers.)

In life, managing time and sticking to schedules, taking into account personalities and expectations of others, is a huge area where control is both sorely needed and yet often evasive. Especially when an "early" marries a "tardy" and together they crank out three offspring, with only one possessing the "early" gene. (Yes, Mitch and I are unfortunately outnumbered.)

Forget the mice and men, I want *my* best-laid schemes *not* to go awry. I want to chart out my days, weeks, and months according to what I think is sensible. And then I want all the pieces to fall into place so that I won't have to adjust my course, rearrange my schedule, expend time waiting (the worst!), or make last-minute modifications that knock the rest of my day off-kilter, making me frustrated and cantankerous.

Opinion Control

Why do I so long to control time? I've had to drill down deep on this issue and get honest about why I think it's so essential to be punctual, why I hate to waste time, why I loathe waiting. Why, if I'm not careful, I often clog up any calendar white space with even more to-dos. Why the clock and my calendar are yet two more entities over which I want to apply control. Especially when I seem to talk out of both sides of my mouth, crafting "I wish I could just dawdle" domestic fictional scripts.

A hefty chunk of the reason is that in being in control of my time, I can influence others' opinions of me.

And let's face it, women who have control of the clock are viewed as confident and capable, especially by their slower sisters who often struggle to stay true to task.

I've always craved looking capable. My flesh loves to gobble up a steady diet of "atta girls" while stoking and stroking its insatiable ego. And the phrase "Wow, is she able to get things done!" is an atta girl I've eagerly collected for years.

I recognize that craving such an outward appearance is utterly prideful. The Spirit reminds me to find my identity in Christ, not in a façade of capability and certainly not in others' opinions of me. Oh, how difficult this is for an approval-addicted, over-achieving, "gee, I hope she likes me" kind of gal such as I. I must swim crosscurrent and make life choices, not for the crowd, but rather and rightly only — as my Bible-teacher friend Wendy Pope states at the close of all her emails — "for an audience of One."

Yes, wanting to control another's opinion of me by appearing to be an In-Charge Ingrid or a Schedule-Sticking Sally is a foolish and puffed-up ambition.

What other reasons do women have for chasing control of the clock? Because being on time and on task gives us a feeling of authority. We're calling the plays, determining the direction of the day. We feel powerful and important when we are at the helm as the master of our destinies, even if the destination of our day merely involves getting the house clean and errands crossed off our to-do lists. (Has any woman ever actually reached the end of her to-do list? As I near the finish line, I always discover even more chores to add. It really isn't a to-do *list*. It's more like a to-do turnstile!)

As women, we like to see progress and productivity. Is there a worse feeling than flitting about from sunup to lights out only to spy no results, especially concrete ones that will last? My author friend Susan Alexander Yates tells of how, as a young mother of five small children, she once happily (though profusely sweating in the beating-down sun) mowed an entire sprawling lawn just because she knew she would be accomplishing something that would last an entire week without needing to be redone!

We also attempt to whip our families and schedules into shape because we feel it's duly expected of us as the matriarchs of our broods. Moms are supposed to maintain their family's momentum, to keep winding the key on some governing clock

135

so as not to let the ticking decelerate, causing life to come to an embarrassing halt while the rest of society rumbles along, gaining velocity in the race for some invisible (and elusive) finish line.

Yes, moms keep the family migrating, herding them from hurried place to hurried place. Who would dare step a toe out of the chorus line of activity? Keeping in sync is crucial. We must each outdo the other in the busy-buzz of family life. It's the modern way of our culture. Even of our churches.

Crises, Delays, and Interruptions

However — no real shocker here — our best-laid plans don't always come to fruition. Weekly, if not daily, we face delays, interruptions, sidetracking issues, and inconveniences. They may come by way of the phone, an email, or a knock on the door.

Someone has a crisis. So she summons you. And now? Well, her crisis is suddenly now your crisis too.

Or you're thrown a last-minute loop in the form of a sick child who needs caring for or a hurting neighbor who could use a listening ear. Or the washing machine decides to give up the ghost, sending you cross town to the Laundromat. So you must pause. Rearrange. Even opt out of your self-scripted agenda altogether. Yes, ma'am. This unplanned side trip has you steaming.

It isn't always a major interruption in your day that can cause you grief. The minor hiccups can be just as disheartening. A child has a question that pulls you away from the task you're tackling. Juice gets spilled or soup is slopped, requiring your attention. A family member on a different floor needs Mom (no, Dad will not do), and it detours you and threatens to arrest your progress.

If, by chance, your best-laid plans get interrupted or derailed, how do you respond? Do you choose at such delicate junctures to exert the helpful, needful control you *should* seek—that of your tongue? Or do you let it hurl and unfurl, taking out loved ones in its path?

Sippin' Sweet Tea

"She's a big-city southern gal who just happened to be born in a tiny town in the Midwest."

Those are the words I use to answer people who question why our twenty-one-year-old daughter, Mackenzie, chose to move from our little Michigan village and take up residence in Charlotte, North Carolina, to attend cosmetology school just after high school graduation.

Ever since the first time Mackenzie traveled with me as a young teen to a speaking engagement in the south, she was hooked. She loved the food (especially Chick-fil-A, which we sadly don't have in here in Michigan), the weather, the big hairstyles (usually the weather *results* in those big hairstyles!), the ocean nearby, and the regional accent. (Yes, she now refers to others as "ya'll." Unless of course she's talking to more than one person. Then she uses the proper plural form of "y'all," which is—if you didn't know—"*all* y'all.")

But most importantly, my baby girl, when first south of the Mason-Dixon Line, couldn't get enough of southern sweet tea!

Today, when she's cruising around Charlotte in her tan 1999 Buick, she often has a glass of her beloved beverage snugged in her car's cup holder. She can sip her icy tisane while idling at long red lights or inching along in the carpool line as she picks up the kids she babysits a few afternoons a week.

However, when she's driving down the road at normal speed

and has to take a sharp corner, she must hold tight to her beverage cup. Even though it sports a travel lid, her car's cup holder sometimes malfunctions, sending the mug flying onto the floor.

Let me pose a simple question: When she forgets to secure her cup at a corner, or if she were ever suddenly bumped in a fender bender from behind, what would spill out of her travel mug?

Yep. *Sweet tea.*

It wouldn't be old, cold, bitter coffee leftover from three days ago. Nor would it be nasty, sticky, syrupy Mountain Dew with a fly backstroking in it that one of her brothers forgot to dump out the last time he rode in her car.

It would be sweet tea. It could only be what is *already inside* the glass.

Likewise, when someone bumps my day's agenda, threatening to knock the *nice* clear outta me, guess what happens: *What is already inside of me will spill out.*

If I react to my husband with harsh words when he interrupts my time, if I snap at a coworker for her inefficiency on a shared project, or if I answer my offspring's call of "Mom!" for the twenty-seventh time with a harsh, angry, and witchlike "Whaaaaaaat!!" I'm simply spilling out what is already inside.

Read this verse slowly, allowing its words to penetrate your soul: "A good person produces good things from the treasury of a good heart, and an evil person produces evil things from the treasury of an evil heart. What you say flows from what is in your heart" (Luke 6:45 NLT).

A treasury is a place where valuables are collected, managed, and then distributed. Does that not perfectly describe our hearts? We collect thoughts, manage our emotions, and disburse reactions all through the channel of our hearts.

Though I may make excuses for my hideous behavior, reasoning that my pestering kids "made" me snap at them with ugly words and a caustic tone, my response to their questions or interruptions to my day just reveals what is *already* simmering inside me.

Missionary Amy Carmichael first uttered this concept: "If a sudden jar can cause me to speak an impatient, unloving word, then I know nothing of Calvary love. For a cup brimful of sweet water cannot spill even one drop of bitter water, however suddenly jolted."[3]

And a tipped-over glass of southern sweet tea is incapable of leaking anything but the sugary, delightful drink inside.

Let's purpose today to fill our hearts' treasuries to the brim with the sweet, not the bitter, to store up God's words to us in this verse, asking him to bring them to our minds *before* we answer with our mouths in a way that might be awfully ugly.

When we're suddenly or perpetually bumped, jarred, or shaken while attempting to stick to our self-imposed schedules, let's all transform into southern gals and spill ourselves some good ole sweet tea.

Sound good, y'all?

Oops. I mean "all y'all."

Putting the Brakes on Busy

The desire to be in command of our time and on top of our tasks isn't inherently wrong. Wanting to be conscientious is admirable. Managing our time efficiently and productively is honorable, helpful, and even biblical. But as we've explored before, a runaway good intention can often backfire. How do we strike a balance?

When our schedules scream, must we always shout back?

Must we bark out orders to our crew as the decibel level climbs and frustrations amass? What if we stepped off the treadmill of life long enough to do a little evaluation, deciding whether the problem lies in the speed at which we've cranked the machine's dial and the incline we've set for the climb?

Being busy is the new measuring stick of family success. While people in prior decades chased a nice house or a new car, today we spell societal status B-U-S-Y.

Play the sports. Join the committee and cause. Serve the candidate. Help the community. Watch the reality-TV show (so we can be in the know at the watercooler the next day or online yet that night). Hit the special sale. Attend the game. Take the trip. Know the movie stars' names. Attend the concert. Don't miss the thrill of being part of this group and that. At every turn is an activity (many worthwhile) begging and beckoning us to blessed busyness.

Could we dare to silence the screaming by uttering a most difficult, albeit single-syllable word, "No"? Maybe, just maybe, if we got intentional about weeding out commitments and obligations *before* the schedule started its bossy chant, we wouldn't need to seek such control in the first place.

How about trying some of the following countercultural ideas?

Stand back and ask, "Why?"

Not just for you personally, but pose this question to your family members now and often. Don't sign up for every happening without a valid reason. Just because it's basketball season doesn't mean all of your kids must play. Ask the big why. Why do they want to engage in the activity? Is it for love of the game? Or because they're skilled? Or are they seeking participation simply because "everyone is doing it"? (Cue our moms' retro mantra about that infamous overpass. "If he jumped off a bridge …") Are we—or they—participating because of another's expectation? Get to the bottom of the most basic why.

Dare to be different.

Don't succumb to peer pressure, even as an adult. If you don't thoroughly enjoy the activity or feel it needful to participate, opt out. Don't apologize. Fight the urge to join out of a feeling of duty or to impress or please someone else. Stand up and then stand out.

Consider setting number limits.

We have teenage boys who love sports and a daughter who loved both volleyball and theater. We allowed our kids one "free" sport or major commitment per year. After that, they had to put forth some capital. Making our kids invest some cash (or extra chores if money was scarce) helped them differentiate between a desired activity and a pass-the-time, thoughtless habit. The latter were things they really didn't want to do but were jumping in on because of peer pressure or boredom, or because it was a free ride, requiring no cost on their part.

Make a list and check it twice.

Resurrect the old practice of making a pros-and-cons list. Sometimes putting your thoughts down in writing can help you think more clearly and make the right call. Chronicle every reason you can conjure up as to why participation would be beneficial. Now turn the tide and list the drawbacks or concerns. Pray over each list, asking God to help you make the wisest call.

Realize how each family member's activities affect the others' schedules.

Does Dad have a crazy summer at work? Perhaps letting every child in the home sign up for a summertime sport may not be prudent. It may pull the family in too many directions. Does Junior need extra time during the school year to spend on homework for a difficult math class that administers a weekly test on Fridays? Maybe this year the Thursday-night bowling league might not be Dad's best choice if he's the parent with the strongest arithmetic skills who could best help Junior study each week.

Don't take on more than you can pray for.

My friend Becky challenged me with this several years ago. With each club we join or each commitment you say yes to, you'll meet and interact with more people. And you'll have more duties, which will require more effort and time.

You'll naturally want to care for the people, be interested in their lives. This will add to your ever-growing prayer list. So ask yourself, can I add the time needed to pray adequately for these people and responsibilities? If not, consider that it might not be best to take on one more commitment.

Say yes because you feel called, not because you consider yourself capable.

My friend Suzy (can you tell I have lots of wise friends?) once told me this: every need isn't necessarily your calling. Don't chime in with a hearty yes because you can perform the task with ease. Don't agree to sign on the dotted line because you know how to do something. Go before the Lord and ask, "Are you calling me to this?" Then wait till he's spoken. Resist answering in the affirmative unless you know God desires for you to serve, give, lead, or teach in this area. If you don't sense a yes from God, don't give one to the person asking you to fill the role.

Don't attempt to set the world record for most consecutive years served.

Okay, I know. You've been chairwoman of the PTA since your first child started school fourteen years ago. Do you still feel it's what God would have you do? Or are you staying in the position because others are counting on you? Do you feel pressured to continue even though, in your heart, you'd love to step down? Go with your gut (tempered with prayer, of course) and politely end your reign. I hate to break it to you, but they can find someone else. If you suddenly moved two states away, they'd have to replace you. Don't make the move; just decline the invite to continue in this activity, especially if your heart and soul are no longer in it.

Ponder this truth: The less you're involved in, the less your schedule will scream, and the less you just might too.

Often we overcontrol our kids, our schedules, and our surroundings because we feel pressed for time. With no margins built in or wiggle room for when plans do go awry, combativeness and a critical spirit can fester inside of us, spilling out at even the slightest bump, threatening to soak and stain everyone in its path. When we don't feel stalked and chased by our schedules, we're more likely to find a place of calm and order.

Seeking a balance between doing and being is complex. But as my friend Lisa Whelchel reminds me, we're human *beings*, not human *doings*. Perhaps it's best, then, to err on the side of less doing and more being, to spend time in thankful quiet each day before racing and chasing in this hurried and harried culture of ours.

When you're intentional about filling your time and your day planner with only what is necessary and part of your calling, and when you model for your children how to do the same, you might actually have an unhurried day every now and then, the kind you can only dream of right now.

When your schedule screams, and you want to scream too, put a muzzle on it.

Seek margin.

And space.

Ask the tough whys and why nots. Don't let the speed of society be your pace car tempting you to speed ahead of yourself in an attempt to keep up with the Joneses' busy status updates.

Follow instead after the One who said, "But I trust in you, LORD; / I say, 'You are my God.' / My times are in your hands" (Psalm 31:14–15).

PART 3

How to Lose Control
and Keep the Faith

When we clamor for control and grab for order, we often assume that we're doing a good thing. After all, doesn't God help those who help themselves? Doesn't he want us to be proactive? To not sit idly by or be uninvolved? By springing into action, we feel we're being conscientious followers of Christ and doing our part in the kingdom. But what if we're in fact getting ahead of ourselves—no, worse, getting ahead of Jesus? Are our eyes fixed on Jesus or on our own running feet? Can we learn to stop running the show and start walking in faith? Let's find out.

CHAPTER 8

Due to Circumstances beyond Our Control

Circumstances are beyond human control, but our conduct is in our own power.
Benjamin Disraeli, British statesman, 1804–1881

Tear man out of his outward circumstances; and what he then is; that only is he.
Johann G. Seume; German theologian, 1763–1810

Always be joyful. Never stop praying. Be thankful in all circumstances, for this is God's will for you who belong to Christ Jesus.
1 Thessalonians 5:16–18 (NLT)

A ren't you going do something about it?" my friend asked as we sat sipping iced tea on my apartment patio one sweltering July afternoon. "That really isn't fair."

My anger was rising as fast as the mercury on the thermometer hanging on the garden fence. I didn't think it was fair either, but I wasn't sure what, if anything, I could do about the situation.

Our town's annual festival based on our famous bumper crop—mint—was coming up in just three short weeks. Every church in the town had been invited to have one of its members perform a musical number at the city band shell on the Sunday afternoon of the festival in a sort of afternoon Christian concert in the park.

Each pastor had been told to alert his congregation about the opportunity and then see who was interested. Then each church could submit one name (or the name of a duo or trio perhaps) for the concert. Since I had several friends at other churches in town, I knew many churches had already posted a sign-up sheet and taken names on a first-come-first-served basis or held some other draw-names-out-of-a-hat method of choosing. I kept waiting for the sign-up sheet to go up on our church's bulletin board so I could take a shot at participating.

It never did.

Upon further investigation, my husband and I discovered that the person in charge of choosing who would represent our church had an immediate family member who liked to sing in church often, and he had already submitted the name of that person to the festival committee. Case closed.

I wasn't upset that I wasn't the one chosen to sing. I actually had a few close friends who loved performing solos too, and they might have been chosen. What I was upset about was the fact that the selection process hadn't been done aboveboard, and not everyone in our congregation had been given an equal chance to participate.

Todd and I discussed this. Should we confront this person? He most likely didn't know that some of us had been clued in to the situation. Would it affect his view of us? Or jeopardize my husband's job, since he was a church leader? We decided to make an appointment to see this person at his office the following week.

Fiddling with my iced-tea straw, I brought my friend up to speed. "Well, you can pray for me. We're discussing it with him tomorrow. I'm not looking forward to it. I'd rather have a root canal."

I was nervous. Since childhood I've shied away from conflict and confrontation. I didn't want to appear accusatory, but I did want some answers. I also feared that our relationship with our pastor would never be the same.

The meeting came and went. I don't remember much about the powwow, only my husband respectfully asking why and our being told that actions like the one this leader took were "a perk of being in ministry" or something. There were also murmurings of Calvinism versus Arminianism that made no sense to me. We left without a good explanation and with no budging on the leader's part. Normally a very gracious soul, he was rather protective about his loved one and not willing to disappoint them by not allowing their name to be the one submitted.

I tried to put the situation behind me but still bristled when the details crept back into the crevices of my mind. However, during this time God began to deal with me about my need to be in control and my inability to let matters roll off my back when others overcontrol or give themselves (or another person) an unfair advantage.

As I prayed, I sensed God telling me to be quiet. To forgive, forget, and move on. I made progress on some days, but as the date drew closer, I still let it get my stomach in knots.

Then one morning the phone rang. It was a member of the committee sponsoring the city concert. Somehow they had wound up with a few extra spots and wanted to know if I (and one of my singing friends from church) each wanted to take one.

I smiled as I hung up the phone and tried not to gloat. Really I did.

The concert came. The weather and the turnout that day were both delightful. And my friend and I had the satisfaction of knowing we hadn't been given a place in the concert by preferential treatment. Instead, God was the string puller that day.

So that little scenario ended happily ever after. I can point to it as a time when, faced with what I saw as injustice, I responded by doing what I could, being respectful and gentle, and trusting God with the outcome. (I could also give you dozens of other examples of times when I didn't behave that way!) And yes, I know the outcome that time was favorable to me. That certainly made it easier to swallow. However, I hope I would have been equally okay with the opposite results.

Not being able to sing in a concert isn't a huge deal. It shouldn't be something a girl spends time fussing and fretting about. Why do we get our granny panties in a bunch when we don't get our way, even over seemingly trivial issues? Sometimes we handle what we see as unfair situations with calm and grace, and other times we let them eat away at our very souls, destroying our days, burning up brain energy, and sapping our spiritual strength.

Born to Control?

The desire to control isn't inherently wrong. After all, we've been making choices to control our circumstances almost since we were born. We might not think about it in that light, but it's true. While we may begin life with involuntary actions and reactions — we cry if we feel pain or if our stomachs recognize hunger — we soon learn that using some of these actions on purpose can actually get us results.

Ta-da! We learn the skill of controlling.

Sometimes we control with our voices — a laugh or a wail. Other occasions find us using facial gestures to get our own way. What parent doesn't melt at the enchanting sight of their baby's first smile or pick up a child who is sporting that infamous "poor me" pout?

Later we reach for, grasp, and hold tight to items we desire. When we're successful at obtaining the coveted object, we feel pleasure and power. And so the pattern begins of desiring our own way and then inventing clever ways of actually obtaining it.

Babies discover early on that when they have an audience, they may get results with their behavior. No audience? Well, then no more need to perform.

No doubt you've viewed the funny YouTube videos displaying such antics. A tiny tot is pitching a fit, flailing on the floor, thrashing about and wailing like a banshee because he desires something. And, of course, because he knows mom or dad is watching.

When the peekaboo parent ducks out of the toddler's eyeshot, however, the emotional display ceases. (Of course, the camera continues to capture the entire show from a tripod.) When, after a moment, the child spies the parent peering at him again, he resumes the melodrama in an all-out attempt to get what he wants.

As we grow, we discover another fact about making our own choices and thus being in control: it makes us feel happy. It is true of school-age children, teens, and adults.

I remember the bliss I felt when Todd and I purchased our first home. Sure, it was less than a thousand square feet, with only two bedrooms, a tiny kitchen, and an even tinier bathroom. But it was ours. We owned it. No landlord. No ridiculous and restrictive rules concerning hanging and nailing. We could paint, nail, wallpaper, stencil (don't laugh — stenciling was very happening in the 1980s), and rearrange all we wanted. It felt wonderful after four years of dorm living and three years of apartment dwelling to have a say in our surroundings.

You see, not all control is bad. In fact, many experts have identified being somewhat in control as a key component to happiness and well-being. Of course, that isn't to say we can be absolutely in control at all times, but it does support the notion that those who are able to make decisions rather than just living their lives either at the whim of another or left to chance will experience increased feelings of security and contentment.

The benefits of control may even go beyond security and contentment. Those who have studied the behavior of prisoners of war take note of the way prisoners scrape for any ounce of control. While being held captive and forced to perform manual labor and obey their captors' every wish, prisoners would often look for ways to out-think, trick, or even sabotage their tormentors. Essential to their last shred of human dignity, and perhaps even their survival, was the need to have at least some control over their circumstances and destiny.

Most of us don't dwell in such dire situations as prisoners of war do, but at times, difficult situations do leave us feeling trapped. Unemployment. Illness. The rejection of a friend. The death of a loved one. Disillusionment. Divorce. Whether we're facing these very painful issues—or everyday circumstances that don't stack up according to our wishes—how are we likely to respond?

Yep. We revert to our childish beginnings, attempt to control the situation, and if sensing we aren't experiencing success, pitch ourselves a royal hissy fit. It takes God's grace and a good amount of practice to learn the difference between what we can control and what we need to let go of.

Pulling Strings

I've witnessed a certain scenario countless times in my two decades of parenting: a mother trying to rearrange circumstances for her child to make him happy or to please herself. It turns out there's a little Wanda Holloway in each of us.

For example, tryouts recently took place at a school where a woman I know sends her teenage son. As a sophomore he secured a spot on the junior varsity squad, appropriate for his age. However, when this mom learned that another sophomore was asked to "play up" and was placed on the varsity team, she became enraged.

So she marched her hoppin'-mad self down to the big brick school and demanded an immediate audience with the athletic director. She ranted and raved about skill level and such until the poor man finally gave in and allowed her son to be placed on the varsity team too. (To get her to stop yakking, perchance?)

Grinning and feeling oh-so-powerful, she returned home to tell the news to her boy, who promptly elected her Make-It-Happen Mom of the Year.

Fast-forward a few months.

The son got a spot on the varsity squad all right. A spot squarely on the bench! While the other sophomore, an outstanding athlete, started and played the whole game, this boy got only occasional time on the field. The rest of the time he spent "riding the pine." Had he (and his shuffle-the-circumstances mom) just accepted the spot he had earned, he would have played all season as one of the stars of the junior varsity team. Instead, he got the thrill of being on the highest-level team (well, not really, since his teammates knew it was only because his mom stomped her feet), but very little time actually playing the sport he loved.

We'll find ourselves more content in the end if we learn to make that choice at the beginning.

Control versus Christ

Those of us who are followers of Jesus Christ must seek the truths found in Scripture about what we should try to control and what we must leave up to God.

In the Bible we're told that it is God who controls many things. One of them is nature:

> Stop and consider the wonderful miracles of
>   God!
> Do you know how God controls the storm
>   and causes the lightning to flash from his
>   clouds?
> Do you understand how he moves the clouds
>   with wonderful perfection and skill?
> When you are sweltering in your clothes
>   and the south wind dies down and everything
>   is still,
> he makes the skies reflect the heat like a bronze
>   mirror.
> Can you do that?
>
> (Job 37:14–18 NLT)

Lest we think controlling the elements was just an act God performed in the Old Testament, stop to consider what is written about the day the disciples were with Jesus on a rough and rocky afternoon boat ride. The waves got a little too choppy for these seasoned fishermen, and they all began to panic, thinking they were surely going to die.

> And they went and woke him [Jesus], saying, "Master, Master, we are perishing!" And he awoke and rebuked the wind and the raging waves, and they ceased, and there was a calm. He said to them, "Where is your faith?" And they were afraid, and they marveled, saying to one another, "Who then is this, that he commands even winds and water, and they obey him?"
> (Luke 8:24–25 ESV)

Okay, not many people, meteorologists included, would assert that humans can control the weather. That one we leave to God. Not many arguments there. We'll leave control of the elements under God's job description. Since we readily accept this truth, we don't beat ourselves up trying to invent ways to make it rain when our lawns are browning or produce sunshine for the family reunion picnic. We accept what we cannot change, and we adjust our actions (and in the weather's case, our clothing) and move on.

But what about our circumstances? Flip on any TV talk show or pick up a book in the self-help section of a bookstore, and you'll see glimmers of this line of thinking prominent in our modern-day society:

If it is to be, it's up to me.

I am the master of my destiny.

If I can believe it, I can achieve it.

I have the power to change my circumstances.

Uh, sorry, no. Most of the time we actually don't.

We can *attempt* to change our circumstances. Sometimes it works, but not always. There are no foolproof, three-step methods for making the bad, or just the annoying, in our lives go away. Usually the only aspect we can change about our circumstances is our outlook. So we must adjust our attitudes, alter our actions, and put on a cloak of contentment in order to weather life's circumstantial storms.

This comes hard. After all, discontent is rampant in our culture. We want something bigger. Or something better. We would rather have her looks or his money. At every turn we slam into that detrimental, "must be nice," nagging discontent.

And apparently it's never more evident than at the local neighborhood hair salon.

As a budding cosmetologist, our daughter greets dozens of clients each week, ergonomic scissors in hand. What strikes me about many of her customers is this: they come to her wanting to be something they are not.

The blondes ask her to make them redheads.

The brunettes want to go several shades lighter, making them almost blonde.

The gals with straight hair come to her for what? Yep. A permanent. (Or as my husband calls them, a "temporary." If they were permanent, you'd only need to get them once!)

And of course, the women with beautiful, bouncy, and tightly curled hair come to the salon to purchase what apparatus?

Uh-huh. A flatiron.

Few of us are happy with the biological hand we've been dealt. But it goes further.

Yes, we want to change our looks, but we also want to change our income levels, our domestic surroundings, the possessions we own. And while we're at it, we might as well swap out our hubby and kids for a more cooperative clan.

But changing our circumstances rarely changes us. What transforms our outlook and us is an attitude shift. It's God's job to determine our circumstances. It's our job to cooperate with him in the midst of them, adjusting and realigning our attitudes with the truth of Scripture.

As the Bible says, "In their hearts humans plan their course, / but the LORD establishes their steps" (Proverbs 16:9). We may set our hearts on what we hope will happen, but nothing happens without God getting his way.

Why, God even uses evil people, with their not-so-nice

intentions, to bring about his will. The Bible is chock-full of such examples. This illustrates the truth found smack-dab in Proverbs 28:10: "Those who lead good people along an evil path / will fall into their own trap, / but the honest will inherit good things" (NLT).

Yes, God's will *will* prevail no matter what people try to do about it. Especially evil men and women. Others may try to alter the situation by behaving badly. In the end, God still gets his own way.

What about our own quest to control other people, especially those who make decisions that directly affect our circumstances? The coach who picks the team. The director who casts the show. The boss who grants the promotions and orders the Donald Trump–like firings. The in-law who oversees the reunion. Even our kids, who affect our happiness by their exemplary or exasperating behavior.

A quick search on a bookseller's website will turn up all sorts of clever titles in this popular area. They deal with winning friends and influencing people, getting others to do what we want them to do, making our children mind, sparking certain performances in our kids or spouses, and other such make-them-behave manuals.

Is it our job to make others mind, behave, or jump on command? If God is so ginormous and grand and in such complete control that whatever he wants will come true anyway, should we mortals even attempt to sway the story line of life at all?

Dare we have a desire or dream and "go for it," or would it be best if we just sit back and let the Creator of the universe unfurl his orders for us while we twiddle our neatly manicured thumbs? For some answers, let's look at the inspiring biblical account of Queen Esther.

Cue the Queen

Esther is the scriptural role model for how to control what you should and trust God with what you can't. And, more importantly, how to decide which is which!

Esther was a stunningly beautiful Jewish orphan who became the replacement for Queen Vashti, the wife of King Xerxes. She had a little help from the man who raised her, her uncle Mordecai, who would become an asset to King Xerxes after saving Xerxes's life by uncovering an assassination plot. However, Esther's Semitic heritage wasn't revealed to the king during the country-wide beauty pageant that was held to select which giddy gal got to wear the queen's sparkly crown.

Though King Xerxes would come to think Uncle Morty was keen, one of the king's officials, Haman, loathed him. He had a prejudice against those who were different, and "that Jew Mordecai," as Haman referred to him, was annoyingly different. You see, Uncle Morty refused to bow down to the narcissistic Haman whenever the official paraded by in all his pomp and circumstance. It enraged Haman. He became so enraged, he cunningly convinced the king to annihilate the entire Jewish population from the face of the earth and then sealed their fate with a stamp of the king's signet ring.

Uh-oh.

Time for *someone* to adjust Queen Esther's crown. Cue Esther's entrance music, please—and fast!

Mordecai was distraught, but he approached his niece—turned daughter, turned queen—to suggest how she might remedy the tragic situation about to ensue.

It was customary in the king's court to only be granted an audience when summoned by His Royal Highness. Even his wife Esther couldn't barge into the hubster's palace office and declare, "Hey, honey, can I talk to you about something?" Oh no. Doing such a thing didn't just have the potential of ticking off her spouse; it could cost the queen her very life. And—not that she had it documented in her day planner—Esther realized she hadn't been called for in more than thirty days. The queen was in a quandary. What was she to do?

Esther gathered her courage, and she also gathered her maidservants and all the Jewish people of Persia to fast with and for her for three straight days. Then this brave and humble woman approached King Xerxes—*gasp*—without being called. He miraculously extended his scepter (instead of ordering, "Off with her head!") and even asked her what it was she wished. He would willingly grant it—up to half of his kingdom.

She asked for a banquet or two (even gals back then loved to throw a good party), and it was as good as done. The first was with her and the Mr. and that third wheel Horrible Haman. After the feast, Haman began building a gallows fit for his enemy Mordecai, who was soon, along with the rest of the Jews, to be toast.

That night the king—suffering from a little insomnia—called, in the wee hours of the morning, for the history books to be opened (since all the Persian drugstores were closed). The account of Mordecai unearthing the terrible assassination plot and saving the king's life was retold. The king discovered he'd never even thanked the guy. So he asked his palace pal Haman what should be done for someone whom the king wanted to honor. Haman, the self-centered man, thought the king must surely be speaking of him and suggested a little parade through town wearing fine clothes, riding upon a royal horse, with all the townsfolk bowing down to him in adoration.

He nearly expired when Xerxes told him, "Well, then. Go do exactly that for Mordecai."

Double ouch.

Though completely humiliated and dejected, Haman obeyed.

At her second banquet, Esther revealed to the king the coming genocide of the Jews, along with the fact that she was one of them.

"Who would order such a thing?" Xerxes demanded to know. When he learned it was Haman, he went out to the palace gardens to let off a little steam. Upon returning, he happened upon Haman and Esther. Haman was lying across the couch on top of the queen, pleading for his life. King X, of course, thought Haman had something X-rated on his mind.

He immediately ordered Haman be hung on the gallows — the ones Haman thought he'd see his enemy Mordecai dangling from — and promptly promoted Uncle Morty to prime minister.

The horrible homicide plan against the Jews was halted, and they were allowed to live and defend themselves from all enemies.

Throughout this whole reality-TV-type drama (the first scene with the gals all lined up hoping to be selected queen, an ancient episode of *The Bachelor*, perhaps?), Queen Esther remained focused and clear. What can we learn from her that will guide us as we navigate our own life circumstances, whether dire or humdrum? Following are some helpful lessons we can glean from Esther's life.

Remember God is God and you are not.

When stuck in the muck of less-than-lovely circumstances, our first — and sometimes only — aim is to get ourselves out, and fast. With this line of thinking permeating our action plans, we can readily forget that we are not the ones in charge. Without a proper perspective, we face frustration. We try our level best to modify the circumstances, but we can't always get people to change their minds to our liking. We can't shoo away the sickness or ward off the altercation. But we should, like Esther, learn our place. We are human, not deity.

When we even subconsciously think we can control the situation and the outcome but fall short, we may succumb to situational depression. We must remember that God is God and we are not. We must look to him for our role in the scenario being played out. How should we respond? What should we do? How should we pray? We must not, however, attempt to take his job away from him. That choice never ends well.

Pray, and if you must, fast.

Queen Esther, though a royal family member, didn't just proceed with the recommended plan; she sought after God. Before leaping into action, she paused. A three-day fast gave her time to draw near to God and sense his assessment of the sticky situation at hand. Should she have decided on her own in a blink and not in a God-bathed response, she might have made a misstep. But because she sought God first, she was infused with his direction and ready to take the right steps that would lead to a resolution of the looming doom.

So pray before you act, and fast from food if God calls you to (check with a medical professional if there are conditions that would make this unwise for you). You may also fast from other things—like talking on the phone (in a gossipy way) about the people involved in the situation, or from the Internet or TV—so you can devote the time to prayer and Bible reading instead.

Solicit spiritual help.

Esther realized she wasn't a Lone Ranger believer. She sought help. Her fast was a group effort. Her maidservants joined her.

So did the other Jews in her homeland of Persia. She knew that this challenge she faced required a call out to the troops for backup reinforcement.

Our friends who follow hard after God are invaluable allies. Surround yourself with at least a few — and sometimes a slew — who will thunder heaven on your behalf, begging God to move. Caution: Don't just pick a sympathetic friend who will give you an "oh, poor baby" and take your side. Straight shooters are best — those who love you enough to tell you when they sense you're being selfish or unreasonable. My accountability partner, Mary, has given me a spiritual whoopin' more than one time, snapping me back to reality and enabling me to make God-glorifying choices.

Do what you can.

Nothing is wrong with action. Sure, look into options and explore the possibility of doing something, but never without taking the spiritual steps already mentioned. If *after* praying, seeking God, and soliciting wise counsel, you feel some action is needed, it's okay to move ahead. Esther did. Where you can get yourself (and your emotions) in a tangled-up mess is when you act before you pray. Leap before you look. Cart before the horse in a race to your own coveted finish. Yes, do what you can — prayerfully and carefully — but leave the results to God. Your job is obedience. God's job is results.

Don't do what you can't.

Realize the nonnegotiables of circumstances. If you can't possibly make a sickness flee or a loved one stop her destructive behavior, don't waste precious energy spinning your wheels trying. Likewise, don't allow your mind to burn up time dwelling on the can'ts of your circumstances. If you can't change something, drop it and move on.

Decide where to glance and where to gaze.

Esther kept her focus and her eyes fixed on her God and not on her circumstances. When your spinning-out-of-control situation permeates your days, it's easy to let it divert your attention and your eyes off Jesus and allow them to become fixated on the problems at hand. That emphasis is all wrong. As author Mary Southerland, a cyberfriend of mine, said in a recent online Bible study, "Trusting God demands that we learn to fix our gaze on him and our glance on our circumstances."

Know when to move and when to stay put.

At times we see Esther moving forward decisively. Other times she idled, taking no evident outward action. In our make-it-happen culture, it feels very foreign to embrace inaction while waiting for God's timing. That's why you must walk so closely with the King that you know both when he is calling you to quietly trust as he works behind the scenes *and* when he is cueing you to make a move. The world screams, "Well, don't just stand there; do something!" However, sometimes our does-things-differently Creator whispers, "Well, don't just do something ... *stand there.*"

Whether your life contains life-altering crises, out-of-control circumstances, or relatively normal bumps and blips, you must nestle yourself neatly and surrendered into the spot God has reserved for you in it all.

You can't always change your circumstances.

You *can* change your attitude.

You shouldn't seek to micromanage.

You *should* seek to trust God.

Instead of longing for God to change the trajectory of your life's story line, look for his face as you practice your faith at each twist and turn along the way.

No, you can't change the weather.

But you can grab an umbrella.

Lord, may I willingly snuggle up next to you under your wide umbrella of grace and growth in the everyday mists of life and—even more closely—during those times when it thunders and pours. Amen.

CHAPTER 9

Soul Control

God is waiting eagerly to respond with new strength to each little act of self-control, small disciplines of prayer, feeble searching after him. And his children shall be filled if they will only hunger and thirst after what he offers.

Richard Holloway

But the fruit of the [Holy] Spirit [the work which His presence within accomplishes] is love, joy (gladness), peace, patience (an even temper, forbearance), kindness, goodness (benevolence), faithfulness, gentleness (meekness, humility), self-control (self-restraint, continence). Against such things there is no law [that can bring a charge]. And those who belong to Christ Jesus (the Messiah) have crucified the flesh (the godless human nature) with its passions and appetites and desires.

Galatians 5:22–24 (AMP)

One sunny, blue-skied, and white-puffy-clouds kind of June day, I hauled my kiddos down to our church for the annual Vacation Bible School week. The coordinator, my friend Trisha, was clever and fun. The kids excitedly attended the five-day session, since they knew it would be fast-paced and packed with awesome activities. And I, as a mom, knew that among the frolic and snacks and occasional water-balloon fights, they would also be learning some scriptural truths.

This particular Monday morning, before the first session began, my friend was in the workers' headquarters, Sharpie marker and poster board in hand, attempting to arrange the children — more than one hundred of them — into "tribes" for the week. I was running registration out in the entrance of the building and had just delivered some late sign-ups to her so she could place them in groups.

When I entered the room, I could see we had ourselves a situation. A hover mother was in the room, although she wasn't a worker and wasn't supposed to be there. She stood peering over Trisha's shoulder, telling her which kids to place where. She wanted to make sure her little "Tommy" got in a tribe with both his older brother and two specific friends of theirs.

Now, had the boys been brand new to the church and known no one else, the request most certainly would have been granted. But their family had been in the church for nearly a decade and knew almost every kid present. Trying to make all the children happy by allowing them to handpick their groups would have been a logistical nightmare!

When it was explained that the boys would just have to go with the group to which they had already been assigned, the mom got visibly irritated. "I want my boys together and in the same group as their friends," she insisted.

Trisha herself was getting steamed at being pulled into this hectic last-minute task as the crowd of kids sat cross-legged in the opening room anxiously waiting for Bible school to kick off. She politely but firmly repeated the policy.

Then Control-Freak Frieda took matters (and practically the Sharpie) into her own hands. She figured out what would make her plan work and then mumbled something about no one telling her what her kids could and couldn't do as she huffed off to tell her boys which group to go in.

A cluster of moms stood dumbfounded.

Later, back home at lunch, my kids brought up what had

happened. "No fair!" and "Why didn't you make them put *us* with our friends?" were their comments to me.

We then had ourselves a discussion about pulling strings and pulling off such shenanigans as this bossy mom with her steamrolling ways. No, my kids didn't get to be in a tribe with their usual friends that year. And I chose not to make a fuss about it. (This hasn't always been the case!)

As the week progressed, my boys got to know a few new kids in their group. They even wanted to have them over on the last day of the session, since they had grown to like their company so much. By practicing quiet acceptance (or in this case being forced to because Mom didn't intervene), my boys learned a small lesson about how to not micromanage circumstances and instead quietly accept them. And they gained some new friends along the way.

As women, doesn't it often seem right to try to rearrange circumstances so that our loved ones get precisely what they desire? After all, don't we only want what's best for them?

Ah ... there is the real issue. What *is* best? Do we always know? And how do we know the difference between what we should try to control and what we should let go of?

In the Waiting Room

Living in an instant culture where meals can be on the table in minutes — from the prepackaged freezer section to the microwave to "Yum!" — or where seemingly serious problems can be solved between commercials over a thirty-minute time span, we don't like to wait.

Wait to find out lab results or game results.

Wait to be happy, fulfilled, and satisfied.

Wait to be vindicated or rewarded.

Wait to see a desire granted or a hope come to fruition.

But God often places us smack-dab inside the waiting room—on purpose. There we drum our fingers. We scheme and plot. We move and micromanage. All the while trying to control the situation.

Yet fretting and fussing over injustice isn't healthy for the soul. It doesn't remedy the dilemma. It doesn't offer constructive talking points for dialogue. It doesn't speak the truth in love. And it certainly doesn't make our stress levels go down. What plummets is our spirits.

Only when we learn to drop the reins will we finally be able to walk in faith. In the meantime, we attempt to exert control and leverage over people and situations by many clever methods. Let's visit them now.

Outright Action

We've already mentioned this most frequent form of control. It's easy to spot. When life isn't aligning itself in a way we would choose, we jump into action. We make the phone call. Send the email or text. Go to the board or complain to the boss. We try to undo what has been done or get the upcoming decision to fall our way.

When we feel our opinions haven't been taken into account or our thoughts on the matter have been sorely overlooked, we simply feel we must weigh in, giving our unsolicited two cents' worth. Often, certain personality types have this ingrained into their very core.

Have you ever known such a person?

Are *you* such a person?

She simply cannot hold her tongue. If a story is being told, she chimes in with her thoughts. If a situation is being outlined, she has to make a running commentary when all you were doing was dispensing information. You weren't looking for an opinion.

This type of person has language full of shoulds, coulds, and woulds. Can you relate?

"Well, what you *should* have done is . . ."

"Now you *could* do XYZ. After all, anyone with any sense knows the sensible thing to do is XYZ."

"If I were you, I *would* blah, blah, blah . . ."

Did you ask her what you should do? Did you plead with her to tell you what she would do if she were you? Did you solicit her opinion at all?

Often this type of outward control sends others packing. No one likes to be around a bossy, combative, and critical person whose "my way or the highway" demeanor makes her the pits to be around. I don't enjoy spending extended periods of time with such a person. Sometimes even a few minutes with someone like this is excruciating. That's a fact.

Want to know another fact?

Sometimes *I* am that person.

Now, some who know me wouldn't say that's so. In certain situations and social circles, I'm *not* quick to give my opinion or overstep my perceived acceptable bounds. I care in these situations how I come across and don't want to be perceived as a Steamroller Sally. So I behave.

"Please. Thank you. No really, you first." And the whole nine yards.

Oh, sisters, I wish this were always true of me! I'm afraid, however, if you asked some people in my life if they view me as such, you would get a hearty, "What are ya, nuts?"

I'm pushy with my children, telling them what they should

(and shouldn't) do. Or say. Or think. Or buy. Or watch. Or
_____ (insert a couple dozen more verbs!)

Mostly I give my husband the brunt of my opinions, whether he wants them or not. And often they're hurled his way with a "Well, any idiot knows that" delivery for added punch.

I've often wondered why I can hold my tongue and temper my actions with friends, strangers, church folk, and the gals down at the ballpark, but I rifle off my "You shoulda, coulda, oughta" opinions like a staccato string of hot ammo at those who share my home address.

I think I know.

They *have* to love me. They are my family. We're stuck with each other. Others in my life can edge me out if I'm not amiable. So around them, I behave. Not that I'm never overcontrolling with nonfamily, but usually I don't struggle with it nearly as much. Do you?

Of course, there are times and places and ways to let our voices be heard. We come once again to that subtle difference between influence and manipulation! But trying to control a situation or a person just for the sake of control tears down relationships instead of building them up—and our influence is probably lost along the way.

Let's visit another form of control we women often pull out of our pockets.

Subtle Mood Swings

If I pout, he'll give in.

If I give her the cold shoulder, she'll change her mind.

If I imply with my tone and with what I *don't* say, appearing to hold back juicy information, she'll think ill of that person.

If I seem irritated in the tone of this email, she'll apologize.

If I throw a temper tantrum, he'll give me my way so I'll stop.

If I strike the martyr's pose and silently communicate, "No, really, it's okay," the committee will assign me the coveted job for fear of hurting my feelings.

Yes, we women know how to control by the many facets of our moods. When we give off a certain vibe, even without words, we can get others to bend. When we say one thing with our mouths but our demeanors say the opposite, we can control others who aren't onto our games.

Or perhaps, they are onto us. They just want the tomfoolery to stop, and they realize that if they don't give us our way, the foolery will keep going on.

The power we exert by our moods is a weapon we learn early on. (I remember many successes with my childhood pouting. It worked especially well with my softy grandfather.) It can also be very destructive, tearing apart what might otherwise be real, honest relationships based on mutual respect and trust. Instead, our relationships are reduced to cat-and-mouse games that don't glorify God.

When I'm tempted to reach into my emotional bag to choose my demonstrative weapon of choice, I have learned to pray that I won't play games but will be forthright with my words. This does *not* come easily to me. I have to make myself speak the truth in a kind manner rather than play another round of the ridiculous Mom's Mood of the Month game.

Speaking up about my needs feels unnatural at times. Sometimes it seems easier to stomp around the house hoping someone will notice I'm upset rather than admitting, "I need some space. I'm going for a walk." I like a good pity party now and then. (My mood of choice is the pout. I've perfected it over the years, and my husband falls for it often.) But whatever forms our emotional tantrums take, they waste time and strain relationships.

Now, enough about *our* emotions, what about playing to *theirs* — the unsuspecting folks we're trying to manipulate? I'll bet you can guess a great emotion to invoke in another person if you want to get your sweet little way.

Guilt-Laying Trips

Ah, yes ... the old guilt trip. Oh, baby, have we gotten a lot of "make it go my way" miles outta this familiar ploy. No quicker way to get others to change their minds about something or give in to our wishes than to slather on an extra thick layer of gloppy, gooey guilt.

We make our husbands feel guilty when we think they aren't meeting our emotional or material needs. Or if we think they aren't being romantic enough or John Wayne–like, rugged-leader enough. Just bring up another guy (who in your eyes is doing it right) and parade him in front of the Mr. for a guilt-inducing round of the comparison shuffle.

I remember one year when I laid on the guilt extra thick. My poor husband had to listen to me repeat two phrases often that year whenever my birthday, Christmas, our anniversary, or Valentine's Day rolled around. (Why, I probably even badgered him on Groundhog Day!)

To set the mood, imagine hands on hips and that side-to-side head move a gal makes, though her body from the neck down is frozen in a "Don't mess with me" demeanor. Got the picture?

After assuming my most intimidating pose, I let loose with the guilt:

"Richard got Suzy a china hutch."

"Denny bought Rose a minivan!"

Yep, two of my friends got awesome gifts that year from their caring hubbies for one of their special occasions.

I got a new toaster oven. And a new oven mitt.

Lovely.

I made my husband feel guilty because he didn't have the wow factor those spouses did when it came to shopping for the little lady that year. I also — even if subtly — made it known that if he had a little more earning power, he might be able to thrill my soul with a big-ticket item such as the ones my friends received.

Guilt sometimes helps us get our way. That year, all it got me was a husband who was dejected because he couldn't please his discontented lady and felt bad about himself because his job wasn't pulling the figures she thought it should.

Normally I'm very low maintenance when it comes to gifts. I'd actually prefer my family save their money and not buy me anything but make me something instead. But that year, in a keep-up-with-the-Joneses sort of way, I wanted a hubby who was a big spender, and I thought sending him on an all-expenses-paid guilt trip would get me my way.

Yep, guilt is a universal weapon we women use on many unsuspecting victims.

Next, we have a more under-the-radar form of control.

Cloaked Concern

Have you discovered this tactic? This is where you spin the request to make it appear that you have the other party's best interests at heart. Very sneaky and clever. It can make you appear caring rather than controlling.

Try these scenarios on for size:

Spoken to your mother-in-law: "I really think that the dress you already have is fine for the wedding. You look so pretty in it. Save your money. You might need it for another expense."

Truth? "The dress is hideous and outdated, but if I agree that you need a new one, then I'll be stuck spending an entire weekend carting you from store to store until you find one you like, and I have zero desire to do *that*."

Told to your child: "I don't think you should try out. The other boys have played football since fourth grade. This is your first try as an eighth grader, and I don't want your feelings hurt if you don't make the team."

Translation? "It will inconvenience me if you make the team — which you most likely will, considering you're a nearly two-hundred-pound, athletic eighth grader, and any coach who doesn't put you on his team as a lead linebacker would be off his pigskin-covered rocker. It will mean lots of running to and from practice, and eight weeks in a row of Saturdays shot to smithereens sitting in the cold watching a sport I don't understand or care to view."

Me, me, me.

Cloaking our control and masquerading it as concern may get us the intended results. However tricky we may feel when it does, we don't fool God. He sees the motives of our hearts. He knows when our mouths utter one thing and our minds are thinking the exact opposite. So, yes, it may get the me's of our lives taken care of, but it fractures our friendship with Jesus.

If we again just spoke the truth in love (are you seeing a pattern here?), we could remedy the situation.

Tell your mother-in-law you think a new dress would be grand. Also tell her you have a three-hour window next Saturday during which you can take her shopping. If a new one isn't located in that time frame, she'll need to make arrangements for another outing with someone else or opt for wearing the dress she already owns. (To be nice, I'd probably leave out the earlier "hideous" part!)

Tell Junior "Go for it!" and then buck up. Part of being a parent is watching activities you don't love just because you have a child (whom you do love) who wants to take part. (Typed the woman who suffered through two years of soccer when I find more excitement watching paint dry. Sorry, you die-hard soccer moms. I'll stick to the baseball diamond.)

Let's not wrap our control in a clever cloak of concern. We're not fooling God, and in essence, we're being dishonest.

Now comes the grand-pappy of them all . . .

Pulling the "God Card"

Oh, boy, have I seen this on many occasions. Sadly, I've even whipped it out myself a time or two.

You know the routine.

Someone says she has "prayed about it" and "really feels that God" would want something this way or that.

Or she uses language like "The Holy Spirit revealed to me . . ." or "God laid it on my heart to tell you . . ." or even "God spoke to me and said without a doubt you are to . . ."

Who is gonna argue when the name of the Most High is invoked?

I'm certainly not saying that God doesn't reveal directions to us. I would never assert that he cannot "lay something" on my heart or yours. I know he still speaks today. But I'm cautious about situational sayings like these.

I'm not quick to question if God has impressed something upon another person's heart. If she feels God prompting *her* to do something, then more power to her. I'm glad she feels she has gotten an answer that is God's plan for her personally.

What concerns me is when, out of the blue, she says God told her that *I* am supposed to do something. Things like "God said to tell you that you're to choose this or decide that or say the other thing." Especially when I never asked her opinion about the matter!

Now I'm not talking about the times we're soliciting sincere counsel from a trusted, growing, and close Christian friend. I have a few close friends who love me, pray for me and my ministry, and have my best interests at heart. I often take their opinions into consideration and follow their advice. I ask the Lord to show me what he would have me do and to confirm it through my close, praying friends. Most times, the answer I feel he is giving me squares up with what they are saying.

It's an altogether different dynamic when someone approaches us out of nowhere in a "God told me" sort of way to notify us what the Almighty wants for our lives.

Yes, pulling the God card can be the ultimate controlling trick up a woman's sneaky sleeve. And when it's pulled on us, it can be difficult to call it what it is — outright manipulation.

All of the outright and subtle ways we women control are attempts to make us the deity in our lives. I know that seems harsh, but it's true. How can we learn to let go and allow God to run the show again? Let's take a look at someone who, though a former card-carrying member of Control Freaks Anonymous, did just that.

Soul Control

During our eight-month engagement, Todd and I counted out the days before our wedding, figuring when we would have 150 days left. Then starting at 150 days to go, we read the psalm that corresponded to that day. (Although a popular practice, many couples dread the day when there are 119 days to go, since that psalm is so long!)

I had read many of the psalms before that time in my life. In high school I cut my spiritual teeth on the books of Proverbs and Psalms, as well as the Gospels. But reading one psalm each day during this exciting time in my life helped to drive home points of this poetical book I might not have otherwise noticed.

I became familiar with some of the writers of the Psalms. Most notable was King David. Many were anonymous. Other psalms were attributed to Heman and Ethan and the Sons of Korah. Some were written by a man who bore the same last name as my beloved high school US history teacher — Asaph.

I caught on pretty quickly to the fact that the Psalms had to do with music, what with all the talk of ten-stringed lyres and "According to the Doe of the Dawn." I also became acquainted with words like *Selah*, which means "to pause and listen" or "to stop and think of that." (Hey ... maybe I should start saying that to my kiddos when I want them to take note of my instructions to them. "Spencer, it's time to clean your room. *Selah*. And pronto!")

I also saw a recurring phrase pop up in the book of Psalms. Depending on the version I was using, it was either "O my soul" or "My soul."

At first I thought this was just some Old Testament Bible lingo that gave a verse poetic cadence but really didn't add anything special to the verse's meaning. The meaning has magnified, however, as I have grown older and realized that every word of Scripture has a distinct purpose. I've peeled back the layers of meaning on these heartfelt, honest verses. In these beautiful songs, the writers not only expose their souls to the Creator but bid us, through the verses, to do the same.

Take, for example, Psalm 62, penned by David:

A Calm Resolve to Wait for the Salvation of God
To the Chief Musician. To Jeduthun. A Psalm of David.

[1]Truly my soul silently *waits* for God;
From Him *comes* my salvation.
[2]He only *is* my rock and my salvation;
He is my defense;
I shall not be greatly moved.
[3]How long will you attack a man?
You shall be slain, all of you,
Like a leaning wall and a tottering fence.
[4]They only consult to cast *him* down from his high position;
They delight in lies;
They bless with their mouth,
But they curse inwardly. *Selah*
[5]My soul, wait silently for God alone,
For my expectation *is* from Him.
[6]He only *is* my rock and my salvation;
He is my defense;
I shall not be moved.
[7]In God *is* my salvation and my glory;
The rock of my strength,
And my refuge, *is* in God.
[8]Trust in Him at all times, you people;
Pour out your heart before Him;
God *is* a refuge for us. *Selah*
[9]Surely men of low degree are a vapor,
Men of high degree *are* a lie;
If they *are* weighed on the scales,
They *are* altogether *lighter* than vapor.
[10]Do not trust in oppression,
Nor vainly hope in robbery;
If riches increase,

Do not set *your* heart *on them.*
¹¹God has spoken once,
Twice I have heard this:
That power *belongs* to God.
¹²Also to You, O Lord, *belongs* mercy;
For You render to each one according to his work. (NKJV)

What a perfect psalm for us to cling to as an anchor when we feel that situations are beyond our control!

The simple shepherd boy — turned budding and contemplative psalmist — started out the piece as if addressing another person as he declared his steadfast, immovable trust in God (verses 1 – 2).

Then he moved to mentioning the conflict he was experiencing — talking to it in verse 3 and talking about it in verse 4.

Then he added a *Selah* pause to ponder and focus his thoughts, bringing them into alignment with the Lord's.

But perhaps this isn't an instantaneous leap, this quieting and settling of one's soul in the midst of enemies and attack. So David began to talk to himself, perhaps not audibly as my kids sometimes catch me doing, but in his mind and heart.

Verse 5 shows him engaged in an all-out conversation with his own soul, trying to calm and collect it and get it to snap back into its verse 1 frame of mind — the perspective that displayed steadfast trust and utter hope in God, his rock, defense, and salvation.

Then David spoke to the people in verses 8 through 11, telling them where to place their trust (in the place he just repositioned his own confidence, perhaps?). And he inserted another *Selah* intermission after verse 8. (Might we all need a little more *Selah* and a little less fret?)

And finally, in verse 12, David buttoned up the psalm with

a bold observation as he spoke directly to God: "Also to You, O Lord, belongs mercy; For You render to each one according to his work."

By this, he declared that God puts everyone in their place. After musing about enemies, two-faced individuals, and the wicked; after mulling over the actions of others that are out of his control but never too clever for God; after contemplating plainly on the page of Holy Writ for us to see thousands of years later, David tells us that God is in control. Not *those* people.

Well, his situation sounds a bit like ours at times, doesn't it?

Can we take a few cues from David? From this emotional and pensive man who was often also a knee-jerk reaction hothead, an act-before-you-think kind of guy. A plotter who tried to fix outcomes and position people in a way that suited his fancy, with little regard even if it cost another his life!

I can relate so well to David. In fact, when Todd and I underwent premarital counseling, we had to take a personality profile that not only showcased our tendencies, our strengths, and our weaknesses but also matched us with a few characters in Scripture.

I came out as a lovely amalgamation of a David (a conniving murderer) and a Peter (a lying chicken who denied Christ).

Awesome.

Of course, sitting next to me was my beloved, a striking spiritual 1 – 2 – 3 combo of a Joseph, Moses, and Abraham, all pillars of the faith and exemplary men of God, with wholesome Joseph ranking right under Jesus, having no sin ever mentioned in conjunction with his name (though we know there must have been something — pride, perhaps?).

However, my pastor (upon noticing the deflation of my spirit maybe?) was quick to point out that it was only said of King David—and no one else in the Bible—that he was a man "after [God's] own heart" (1 Sam. 13:14). And that Peter, once he stepped up to the plate, became a bold and effective witness for Christ. (*Hmmph.* Take *that* Jo-Mos-braham!)

What transformed David from a control freak who would stop short of nothing to get his own way—even murdering a man so he could take his wife (see 2 Samuel 11)—into a man who was known as someone who was after God's very heart?

I think it's because he learned the fine art of soul control.

Soul control is when we speak God's truth to ourselves.

Soul control is when we recognize that life isn't fair—that others who seem evil prosper, while the righteous seem to flail about.

Soul control is when we pause to remember our place. And God's.

Soul control is learning to idle our brains before we engage our mouths, thereby saving ourselves a boatload of heartache, wounded relationships, and regret.

Soul control is when we stop—sometimes midsentence—and realign our thinking and resulting actions with God's Word.

Soul control is when we finally realize that it is only God who has *sole* control over the universe.

We do not.

And even though it appears that sometimes people, or even Satan, control the situation, they don't.

Soul control is a fresh dose of perspective amid the turmoil of life that can transform a control-freak woman (who has

181

wounded only with her words perhaps, but killed nonetheless) into a woman who, like transformed David, follows hard after God's heart.

> *Lord, when the situations that swarm around me tempt me to overcontrol and underestimate your power, may I pause and speak truth to my soul. And then may I go forth, content in your plans, trusting in your wisdom and willing to accept the outcome. Selah.*

CHAPTER 10

Embracing Your What-*evvv*-er

Everything has its wonders, even darkness and silence, and I learn, whatever state I may be in, therein to be content.
Helen Keller

Contentment is a pearl of great price, and whoever procures it at the expense of ten thousand desires makes a wise and happy purchase.
John Balguy

I have learned to be content in whatever circumstances I am. I know both how to have a little, and I know how to have a lot. In any and all circumstances I have learned the secret of being content — whether well fed or hungry, whether in abundance or in need. I am able to do all things through Him who strengthens me.
Philippians 4:11 – 13 (HCSB)

*P*sst ... I have a little secret.

The Joneses are overrated.

Oh, I know we'd never think that from the way the Joneses strut about — new cars, fancy homes, important jobs, thrilling vacations, and other "gee it must be nice to be them," envy-invoking facets of their earthly existence. But I'm giving it to you straight up. The Joneses are not all they're cracked up to be.

In my mother's day, you only saw the Joneses a few times a week. Maybe you bumped into them on your way into the church as you strolled in wearing your same old humdrum Sunday-go-to-meeting hat. Mrs. Jones? Well, she had a brand-spankin'-new bright-pastel hat on. The Joneses always wore nicer and more costly clothing.

Or perhaps your paths crossed at the school PTA meeting. You know, as you were getting into your dingy old jalopy, they were happily piling into their new, spit-shined Chevrolet.

Word may have reached your ears about the Joneses' fabulous vacation as you hung up your wash on the line and your nosey neighbor gave you the rundown. A trip to Florida staying at a fancy-pants resort. Your family opted instead for rustic camping trips with an occasional budget-hotel overnight, but only if the hotel chain contained numbers in its name.

The Joneses were lurking around the corner, never too far off. They were not, however, right under your nose all day every day.

What a difference a decade (or two or three) makes! The Joneses now perpetually parade in front of our wondering eyes, spewing at us a steady stream of "you must be nice to be us." On our computer news feeds. And smartphones. And on the hundreds of channels of TV we can now get. On Twitter. And *especially* on Facebook.

Can you relate?

This Is Your Life

It's a random Tuesday evening. Supper is finished—take-out deluxe pizza once again. (You just can't seem to get your culinary act together these days.) You glance at the day's mail, still sitting on the cluttered and sticky kitchen counter where you tossed it earlier. In it are bills waiting to be paid and an overdue library book notice. (Drat! Fined again.)

The digital ring of your cell phone startles you. You recognize it as the ring your kids assigned to your combative in-law.

Not in the mood for a Hatfield-McCoy fight, you choose Ignore from your menu of options.

You're waiting for your husband to return home from work so you can discuss with him the call that came from the principal's office earlier that day. Seems Junior thought it hilarious to experiment with firecrackers under the school's bleachers at recess.

To kill a few minutes until you can hold the parental convention, you hop on Facebook. And there you have it: the "look at me!" Joneses and all their profile-picture-perfect lives.

One friend posts: "Homemade chicken fettuccini Alfredo, fresh beans from the garden, and my famous raspberry cheesecake. It's what's for dinner."

The second friend's status scrolls down: "Woo-hoo! Paid off the mortgage. We're now debt-free!"

Still another boasts: "So proud of my Jimmy. Student of the Year *and* the Golden Character Award too. We're going out to celebrate!"

An acquaintance at church chirps through cyber space: "Three closets cleaned out and the kitchen totally reorganized. I just ♥ a tidy home."

Your down-the-street neighbor chimes in: "So thankful for my sweet mother-in-law who is also one of my very dearest friends."

When an archrival of yours from years gone by posts a few snapshots of her skinny, swimsuit-clad self with her model-like family members on extended holiday in Hawaii, you've had it.

Yes, the Joneses can invade your home and your thoughts several times a day through social media and the Internet.

Even reading blogs can make you unhappy.

Though I love the ministry that can happen with websites and blogs providing ideas, inspiration, and connection for women today, I'm also cognizant of the fact that social media has enormous potential for causing despondency.

Why?

Comparisons.

Comparisons always deal an arresting deathblow to your contentment.

When you see others owning, enjoying, being related to, or experiencing what you don't have but wish you did, it may make you discontent. And discontentment can effortlessly morph its sneaky little self into overcontrol.

"Why can't you ever win Student of the Year instead of the award for 'most visits to the vice-principal's office'?"

"You never take our family on exciting vacations. When are you ever going to have the nerve to finally ask your boss for that raise?"

"Can't you kids help me keep things picked up around here? I'm tired of living in this pigsty. And by the way, I'm your mom, not your maid."

"I can't stand my extended family. Or my too-small kitchen. Or my dead-end job. Or my uninteresting life."

Blah, blah, blah, blah, blah . . .

We compare and covet and desire to make a change or two in our homes or careers or families or looks. To make it happen, we kick the control feature of our personalities into turbocharged overdrive. Yes, catching up with the Joneses is a never-ending run on the treadmill of dissatisfaction.

I know this to be true.

I Want to Be Someone Else

For much of my life, I have been an envious person. While outwardly I seemed happy-go-lucky and content with my lot in life . . . secretly I often wanted to be someone else.

Just after my college days, when I married my college sweetheart three weeks after graduation, I soon became envious of others who seemed to have marriages that were a breeze. The couples got along famously. At my little abode ... well ... not so much. There were cutting words and cold shoulders and numerous newlywed battles. Two babies of the family trying to form a brand-new family wasn't a pretty sight.

As it became clear that my fairy-tale marriage wasn't so "happily ever after" after all, I wanted a different husband — anybody's husband but mine. I desired a romantic, spontaneous, and creative lover. I got Mr. Practical, whose idea of a romantic gesture was emptying the dishwasher, and whose creative birthday present to me was to give me his punch card from the record store where he had earned a free album or new-fangled CD. I wanted a man who would talk to me about my problems in an "oh, poor baby" lengthy discussion centered on me with lots of verbal affirmation instead of a quick fix-it answer to my dilemma centered only on remedying the problem at hand. And I wanted a man with a normal nine-to-five schedule, not one with an inconvenient afternoon shift.

When I became a mom, I had the exact blueprint for what my family would look like. I wanted at least six kids. I was only able to have three. And it soon became obvious that the three I wound up with were simply not following the blueprint. They just didn't quite have the personalities I'd ordered.

My daughter, in my plan, was *supposed* to be an old-fashioned, Laura Ingalls–like, violin-playin', domestic princess. She was, until about the age of eight, when she developed a love of bell-bottoms and contemporary hairstyles. And she developed a quick, sometimes sharp tongue, just like her mother. Suddenly she just didn't quite fit the mold in our circle of friends any longer, and I felt like a failure.

Then our first son came along. And by the middle of third grade, he was still struggling with reading even the simplest words, and we discovered that he is dyslexic—a terrifying word, especially to a homeschool mom. It meant expensive reading therapy and lots of extra time spent on school when I could have had some time to myself like a lot of other moms I knew did. So I threw myself a pity party.

Next, the baby of our family arrived. And out of my body that day shot a strong-willed, in-your-face, spitfire son, which was definitely *not* what I'd ordered. I wanted a mild-mannered, agreeable kid, like all ten of my friend's children. Yes, I have a friend with ten laid-back buckaroos. I just asked for one! How hard could *that* be, God?

To others, my life looked good. Slowly, as the kids grew older, I became a speaker and a published author, but even reaching my writing and speaking dreams came with pain. Because due to my fluctuating weight in my adult and baby-producing years, I sometimes wore a size 10, but most of the time I hovered around a 14 or 16. And for a few years, I even tipped the scales to the point where I barely fit into a size 24.

Around that time I became known as "that funny, fat speaker."

As more speaking opportunities came, I often felt insecure appearing alongside notable, top-notch, "real" speakers, which I feared I wasn't. And I compared myself to these women in my head all the time.

I wrongly surmised that they had it all together. That their lives and families and homes must be perfect, while mine was not.

And as for appearances, well, in that arena I just couldn't compete.

Some of them were a size 2 or 4. Back then I wore a size 24.

They had tan skin and white teeth.

I had white skin and tan teeth!

I decided I just didn't want to be me any longer. I wanted to be someone else.

About that time, my mom brought over a box of things from my childhood. There were school trinkets and Avon perfume bottles and some teenage jewelry pieces. As I perused the box's contents, my eyes became locked on a white-and-gold book — my still-locked-up diary I had kept in sixth grade. And I discovered as I turned the miniature key and flipped through the yellowing pages that my problem wasn't new. Even as a young girl, living in a broken, often empty, and sometimes violent home, I had wanted to be someone else.

January 10, 1976. I went to Judy's slumber party tonight and for supper her parents took us to McDonald's. It was pretty fun. I decided something. From now on I am going to be more like Stephanie.

January 17, 1976. Snow day! No school today. What a bomb. Family Affair is on now and I am watching it. I think I want to be more like Cissy.

January 20, 1976. I cannot believe it!! Tricia said "Bye, Karen," when I got off of the bus. She is the most popular eighth-grader ever. Tonight we had catechism, and I decided that from now on I want to be more like Tricia, and Kay, Kelly, Bonnie, and a lot more girls that I know. That is what I'll do. I'll be like them.

Comparisons Are Odorous

May I suggest, girlfriends, that our discontentment and our desire to control and change our circumstances go back even further than junior high. They go back to our mother Eve and the garden of Eden. The woman who looked around at all God had given her and still wanted the one thing he said she couldn't touch. Disgruntled, she set out to get it.

We still do. We compare our reality with the perception of someone else's perfection. We compare our "yuck" with someone else's seems-to-be "yay!" We compare our boring and familiar with someone else's breathtaking and fabulous.

Compare. Compare. Compare.

I think the great playwright William Shakespeare said it fittingly in his work *Much Ado about Nothing*: "Comparisons are odorous."

He was actually having his character misquote a popular saying of the day, "Comparisons are odious" (meaning hateful), but the character said "odorous." You know what odorous means? They stink! And if we wallow in comparisons long enough . . . we begin to stink.

Whatever!

In a letter to the church in Philippi, the apostle Paul penned these words:

> I have learned to be content in whatever circumstances I am. I know both how to have a little, and I know how to have a lot. In any and all circumstances I have learned the secret of being content—whether well fed or hungry, whether in abundance or in need. I am able to do all things through Him who strengthens me. (Philippians 4:11–13 HCSB)

Now, when did Paul say we should be content? When life is clipping along with everything going our way? When we've just told Howie we'll take the deal? No, it says, "In any and all circumstances."

Just think of Paul writing from a dark, lonely, first-century prison with no Internet access or air-conditioned exercise room.

No iPod with the latest podcast downloads from the Jerusalem radio station WGOD. Yet in the midst of dire circumstances, he claimed he had learned the secret of contentment. He had discovered how to stop trying to control his situation and trust God in the core of whatever life threw his way. His secret was knowing he could do all things through Christ.

The Greek word rendered *content* in this passage denotes more than just a throwing up of one's hands in reluctant acceptance. As when a teenager of today says, shoulders shrugged and eyes rolling, "Okay ... like ... what-*evvv*-er!"

That wasn't the kind of "whatever" Brother Paul was speaking about.

At its hub, the Greek word rendered in today's English as *content* literally means this: "to be satisfied to the point where I am no longer disturbed or disquieted."

This, sisters, is the place God has already prepared for us in the midst of life's storms. He is longing for us to take our eyes off of our situation and fix them solely upon him.

When we adopt this attitude, we live aloud the truth I once heard Elisabeth Elliot declare: "The difference is Christ in me. Not me in a different set of circumstances."

Yet our human minds reason that the exact opposite is true. You know those audio reels that play through your mind: "If only I had her money or her good looks or his brains ..." We're tempted to buy the old lie, "The grass is always greener on the other side of the fence."

No.

Ask any seasoned turf-grass specialist (I'm related to one), and he will tell you this truth. The grass actually has the best chance of turning out Kermit-the-Frog green when it's frequently fertilized and habitually hydrated, and when the pesky, deep-rooted, and often recurring weeds are intentionally pulled out. That's where you'll discover the softest, greenest, thickest grass of all.

Playing the "if only" game and constantly longing to keep up with the Joneses sets up a pattern of disappointment and an urge to control in an attempt to snag ourselves a replica of someone else's seemingly wonderful life.

Ask Yourself This ...

How about turning the tide? In the future, when you're tempted to compare or when you want to weasel out of life's circumstances, stop ... and then quit struggling to alter the circumstances. Instead, ask yourself a few questions like these:

- What does God want me to learn about him that I might never discover if he were to suddenly pluck me out of this situation?

- What Christlike character traits is he trying to grow in me—patience, trust, compassion, faith?

- Who is watching—either up close or from afar—and discovering what God is like by my reactions to my current situation?

- How might my empathy for others deepen if I go through this current trial with grace and acceptance?

- What is God trying to say to me, not by the outcome, but through the voyage?

Learn to be thankful in the midst of your unique "whatever" rather than trying to control something you were never meant to control in the first place. You see, God is more concerned with your attitude and your obedience in the role in which he has presently cast you than he is about giving you a starring role in life. It may be act 1, scene 3 in your life, and you're playing a bit role. Later you'll have a bigger part. But right now God is evaluating your current performance.

This is where many of us get stuck. We're looking for the next step. The bigger platform. The larger home. The better job. The resolved crisis. The accepted application. "Come on, God. What is the next step?"

Maybe there isn't one right now because God is waiting for us to learn what he's trying to teach us on the step we're currently on. Until then, no more marching orders.

First, we have to let go of control and grab hold of our faith.

We need to stop tweaking and trying. Instead, we must start trusting.

It's our job to obey God today, in our current lot in life. It's God's job to grow our careers or our families or our home businesses — if he wishes. It's his job to orchestrate the details. It's our job to watch them fall into place and then move when and where he tells us. It's our job to pray until we get a clear direction. It's God's job to answer our deepest, heartfelt wishes with a resounding "Yes!" if that's his will. Our job is obedience. God's job is results.

No two ways about it. True godly contentment is unavailable in microwave form; it needs to be patiently and purposefully cultivated. We must cease making odious and odorous comparisons and instead embrace our current lot in life — our past, present, and future — welcoming all that God will teach us through it.

Only then we will discover the secret Paul knew — that true

contentment isn't merely having what we want; it's wanting nothing more than what we already have.

So let me ask you, what do you already have?

Simple Snapshots

Today, if you were to see a snapshot of my family, you would see a middle-aged mom and a bald-as-a-cue-ball dad; a twenty-one-year-old, brunette daughter; a seventeen-year-old, auburn-haired son; and a strapping fourteen-year-old boy with a buzz cut so short you can't tell what color his hair is. But if you were to gaze deeper, you would see what I see. And you would understand why God did me a favor by not following the blueprint I had laid out for my family. Because by not giving me what I wanted, he gave me what I needed.

Now I see our somewhat spunky daughter, Mackenzie, is a straight-shootin' fashion plate, who loves people and longs for them to have a real relationship with God and not just play church. She grew up and exchanged her braids and violin for leading worship vocally and theatrically. I love helping her read the blueprint that *God*, not me, is laying out for her life. I now realize that I needed her as my daughter to teach me to stop being a control freak, embrace my kids' unique personalities, and love unconditionally.

Our seventeen-year-old, Mitchell, is a left-handed-pitching, clean-up-batting neatnik who still struggles with schoolwork. But like so many other dyslexics — including Thomas Edison and Albert Einstein — Mitchell has a brilliant no-need-to-read-the-instructions mind. And I love helping him read the blueprint that *God* is laying out for his life. I now realize that I need him as my son to teach me to give unselfishly of my time to my family first before giving it to a ton of other activities outside my home.

And our fourteen-year-old, rambunctious caboose, Spencer, still tries my patience daily, but he also completely cracks me up. And gives me some of my best speaking material!

Like the day when he was five and was sent to his room to think for a while about what offense he'd committed. I ended my directions to him by pulling his bedroom door closed and saying, "And don't you even think about coming out of that door, young man."

About a half hour later, I caught a glimpse of a boy happily playing in our backyard. As he turned to come up on the back deck, I realized it was Spencer. In his eyes, he had obeyed my words completely since I had never told him he couldn't *climb out the window*!

I came unglued, doling out a long list of consequences, ending my rant with, "And that means bad news for *you*, bucko."

Without missing a beat, he looked me in the eye and said, "Oh, really, Mom? Well, there is some good news. Dad just saved a boatload of money on our car insurance by switching to Geico!"

Then there was the summer we had a little medical scare at our house. My husband suddenly lost more than 90 percent of his hair. Just fell out in chunks. During that scary time of medical testing, the kids and I worried and prayed a lot. One night, while tucking Spencer into bed, I sensed his concern, so I said, "Whatcha thinking, buddy?" He began to cry and said, "Mommy, what will we do if Daddy has cancer and dies?"

I assured him that if that did happen, God would see us through. He wiped his tears and said, "Really, Mom? He would? Well, I don't want Daddy to die ... but Mom ... if he does ... would you ever consider going out with Taylor Hicks?"

I am serious.

I love helping Spencer read the blueprint *God* is laying out for his life. I now realize I need him as my son to teach me that sometimes I need to knuckle down and other times I need to lighten up.

My husband, our house, the furniture we own, the cars we drive (our fleet's odometers currently read 148,000, 198,000, and 247,000 miles!)—they all are on purpose, part of my unique "whatever." When I fixate my eyes on the "what could be" and take them off of my "whatever," the comparisons kill any hope I have of dwelling calmly in contentment.

Unlike Paul, who learned to live in plenty or in want, if we compare, we won't discover how to survive and how to thrive in the center of less-than-perfect. We won't joyfully display to others the secret of contentment that Paul knew and lived. And it will make each of us a frustrated, fretting mess of a woman.

Learning the Secret

Let's key in on one word in Philippians 4:11–13 that's easy to gloss over. Paul stated that he learned the *secret* of contentment in the middle of his "whatever." Learning suggests that contentment doesn't come naturally; we weren't born knowing instinctively how to do it. Learning means we have to be taught, maybe even over and over and over again until we get it right. Learning means there are others who might know better how to do it. We might need them to teach us. Learning takes time. We won't do it perfectly on our first attempt. In fact, we must not even seek perfection; we must aim instead for progress.

Each time it just might get a little easier as we learn to hone our skills at living the let-it-go life. But we must recognize the most important truth — relying on the Secret Holder, who gives us the strength and empowers us to change.

Could we do it? Learn to embrace our unique "whatevers"? Become skilled at staying calm and looking for Christ rather than just looking for a way out of our "now" and onto the next bigger, better thing? Could we display to a watching world an attitude that accepts and embraces instead of one that argues and bristles and bucks?

I'll bet we could do it. If we learned to live like the secret is true — the secret of contentment and this secret too: Don't try to keep up with the Joneses. They're overrated.

Keep your eyes firmly fixed on God, not on your circumstances and not on your neighbors. And as you do, remember this truth that I've had to learn the long, hard way: it's better to strive to be an original and unique version of yourself than to try to be a cheap, knock-off imitation of somebody else.

And that starts by embracing your divinely assigned "whatever."

Your whatever looks.

Your whatever income level.

Your whatever possessions.

Your whatever house.

Your whatever spouse.

Your whatever life.

Your one-of-a-kind, exclusive "whatever the circumstances."

Paul would be so proud.

And I'm sure God will smile too.

Father, may I learn the secret Paul knew and live it well. I want to be content in whatever circumstances you place me instead of trying my best to wiggle out of them. Teach me to look for you in the midst of what might seem a less-than-lovely situation. I want my heart to no longer be disturbed or disquieted but instead to be confident in and content with you and you alone. I know you already know what is best for me. Help me to see and know it too. Amen.

CHAPTER 11

Living the Relinquished Life

Sometimes you have to let go to see if there was anything worth holding on to.
Anonymous

I will say of the Lord, He is my Refuge and my Fortress, my God; on Him I lean and rely, and in Him I [confidently] trust!
Psalm 91:2 (AMP)

The maple sleigh bed in our guest bedroom sports a brand-new comforter set. It's something I never would have chosen. In fact, I think it's rather ugly. But the funny thing is, I love walking by the room and spying that spread, because it's a visual reminder to me of the work God has done in my heart.

A few years back, I was speaking at a Hearts at Home moms' conference. There to lead a few workshops and act as the day's emcee, I had the honor of introducing the keynote speaker for the morning. If you are as old as I am, you'll remember her from watching television in the late seventies and early eighties. The younger crowd may remember catching her sitcom later in syndication on TV Land.

Lisa Whelchel (aka Blair on *The Facts of Life*) was the presenter that crisp fall afternoon. Having appeared at a few events together over the years, she and I were becoming friends, and it was my delight to give her intro. After I handed the microphone to her, I settled myself in the auditorium seat, eager to hear what she had to share.

The other times I'd heard Lisa speak, she talked about her life in Hollywood or shared funny and touching stories from her current starring roles as wife and mom. This day, however, she had a strange twist to her talk. Her topic? "The Great Thing about Being Out of Control."

As she spoke of her marriage—much like mine—to a naturally serving, giving, behind-the-scenes husband, paired with her own take-charge personality, I laughed and identified. I had absolutely no idea I was about to get hit with a spiritual two-by-four smack upside my bossy little head.

She challenged the women in the audience to do what she had done the previous year: go on a fast. No, not from food. This type of fast was much more difficult. She dared us to fast for a week (or maybe even longer) from making any executive decisions and getting our own way in our marriages and families.

When Lisa felt God calling her to this little out-of-control exercise, it landed right smack-dab in the middle of the holidays. Still, she sensed strongly that she wasn't to try to micromanage and control but was instead to defer to her husband and his wishes with family decisions.

Like many of us, she normally was a tad on the control-freak side about lights and decor during the holidays. She was a mom whose job it was to pick out the annual family Christmas photo from among the many choices (selecting the one where she looked beautiful and the kids were adorable, and her husband, Steve, at least had his eyes open!).

It nearly made her expire when, during her self-imposed fast, her husband called to say he was picking up new lights to deck the house. He wanted to know what color to get. Or should they be clear?

She bit her tongue and answered, "You decide."

Now, Lisa was of the strong opinion that a home with children should have a spectacular display of all-out bright colors. Uh-huh. You're one step ahead of me. He waltzed through the door that day with bags upon bags of plain, clear lights.

She said nothing. Her home blinked brightly of plain white that year.

An Out-of-Control Christmas

Lisa's message, though comical at times, struck my soul deeply. I wondered if I should try her letting-go experiment. However, I didn't know if I could do it. I knew deep inside that I was even more of a control freak than she. I had serious issues. My domineering ways weren't just humorous fodder for a talk; they were downright harmful.

Still, through her message, I heard God speaking to me. So I whispered a prayer and jumped in, ready to experience the thrill of being out of control.

I am not gonna lie. It was one of the most difficult and frustrating things I have ever done.

EVER!

My fast, too, took place during the yuletide season.

Fantastic.

It soon came time to embellish our house for the holidays. Our young son Spencer, a creative and artsy sort, loves to help with this. His older siblings weren't available to assist that year, so the two of us grabbed the boxes from storage and headed outside to drape the bushes and porch in a display of Christmas splendor and then to aim the spotlights and settle the old-fashioned decorations in their proper places.

Being a woman who thinks life goes along best with

organizational methods in place, I have our big plastic bins of holiday decorations labeled and neatly arranged. My husband meticulously rolls up the lights each January, and we strategically stack the bulbs and bows in their corresponding chambers. Our methodical system makes it a breeze to pull out the items and place them in their preassigned spots on "deck the halls" day.

That is until I was on a decision fast and decorating the place with an all-over-the-map, spontaneous twelve-year-old.

Spencer wanted to place all colored lights on the bushes — the bushes for which I had carefully purchased the exact number of strands of white bulbs, which were waiting neatly rolled up in the box and fastened shut with zip ties. But no, he wanted color.

So I smiled (at least outwardly) and said, "Sure!"

He grabbed some strands (some big lights, some tiny, some twinkling, some not) and draped and dropped the lights on the bushes, not being careful to wind them in an upward and logical way while spacing the rows equidistance apart as any good card-carrying member of Control Freaks Anonymous would do. It looked like a huge handful of colored confetti had been tossed helter-skelter on my front bushes, much of it landing in huge, knotted clumps.

Next he twisted some white lights just halfway up our corner cedar bush. Then he stopped without putting another strand on the top half. He thought it was "different" and would look "supercool."

What? No sane woman lives in a house with lights donning only the bottom half of a huge cedar bush.

I guess I am now officially declared insane.

Then Spencer wanted the antique sled on the right side of the garage door. (I think it looks best on the left, where folks will pass it on the way to our front door.)

He wanted some of the lights to flicker and others to stay on at all times. And there wasn't any rhyme or reason to which strands blinked and which did not.

I told him we had a small budget to purchase a few new items. He was in his glory. While I would have gone downtown to my favorite antique shop to hunt for a retro plastic snowman or a turn-of-the-century holiday postcard or two to toss on our coffee table, he thought we should whip down to the Family Dollar. Once there, he picked out the cheapest, most hideous lighted plastic candy canes I'd ever seen to line our front walkway.

The expensive paper-bag-like luminaries that usually line our tastefully decorated walk — in keeping with the old-fashioned and quaint bed-and-breakfast theme — sat untouched that year in the bottom of a bin.

To add insult to injury, I allowed him to also have his own way with the family Christmas tree.

Yes, I did.

For years we'd had two trees. One stood in our living room, a display of gold-and-plum, shimmering ribbons and glistening orbs nestled among the pearl-white lights, perfectly matching our living-room decor in a way that just screamed HGTV. The kids got to decorate a second tree in the basement family room any way they liked.

Now living in a different house, we had downsized to one tree. On that tree went all of the mismatched ornaments and assorted trinkets Spencer could find. They weren't spaced out evenly. Several bulbs of one color were clustered too near each other for my taste. There were holes where no ornaments hung. I wanted so badly to correct his placement choice, but I didn't. (My mind drifted back to my childhood days when my own

203

mother insisted that the silver tinsel strands be hung a certain way—one by one, separated and not clumped. I always hated that, and I was glad I remembered how I'd felt so I kept my trap shut.)

At the end of the day, we plugged it all in. I don't know which was brighter, the lights or my son's smile. I fixed my little guy some hot cocoa and me a cup of coffee. As I sat next to him on the couch in the glow of the tree, I'd like to say I willingly accepted this new holiday look.

I did not. Instead, I schemed what I could say that would make him allow me to tweak the decorations *just* a bit. Then, in between "The Chipmunks Song (Christmas Don't Be Late)" and "Grandma Got Run Over by a Reindeer" (Yes, the kids got to choose the Christmas music too. Forgive me, Josh Groban!), all at once, he piped up.

"I love you, Mom. Today was the funnest day ever."

My heart both melted and sank—melted at my grateful and content child who, in that moment, captured the wonder of Christmas. Yet my heart sank when I thought of how decorating had often gone at our house years before.

Bossiness. Sharp words. Rolling eyes. Harsh instructions. All from me.

Hurt feelings. Crushed spirits. Dashed hopes. Shot-down ideas. All from my loved ones.

In the end, I may have gotten a magazine-like display, but there was no beaming clan sitting in the midst of the glowing home. They'd all split the seasonal scene.

At that moment I decided there were benefits to being out of control. Sure, the house may not have looked as I'd liked. But my son looked at me with thankfulness and had a sense of real accomplishment and acceptance in his soul.

It was a powerful turning point for me.

The rest of that Christmas season, I stuck to my fast. We rented holiday movies I wouldn't have picked out. We baked cookies that weren't the traditional ones I thought simply must be on the menu. And speaking of menus, the family chose to eat deep-fried chicken sandwiches with honey-mustard sauce and waffle fries for our Christmas dinner that year instead of the traditional ham or turkey. (We don't have Chick-fil-A restaurants here in Michigan, so they love for me to make them mock Chick-fil-A meals reminiscent of the eatery's famous chicken sandwich.) They even opened their stockings last on Christmas morn. Before, I'd always insisted they be opened first — the . . . ahem . . . *right* way.

It was the most wacky, and yet wonderful, Christmas season ever.

Lisa was right. There is something wonderful about learning to live life out of control, to loosen our grip, to not always get our own way, to defer to others and watch their delight as they get to have some of the say for once. It yielded several fantastic results for me.

I wasn't on edge.

I wasn't so bossy.

My family relationships were calmer.

My kids' contributions were endearing to me.

My husband seemed like a hero when I backed off and realized he does have some good ideas.

It was less work for me not always having to be in control.

And most of all, I finally felt the thrill of living relinquished instead of living tightfisted all the time. It required more prayer. And more faith. And a little duct tape for my old mama mouth. But it was a huge life lesson for me.

Allergic to Microsuede

Several times since my little experiment, I've been intentional—when every fiber of my being screams to take charge—to let it go instead.

The most recent example?

That unsightly comforter that adorns the bed in our guest room.

The hubster picked it out.

You might not think it's awful. It probably really isn't. It's a large patchwork pattern of baby blue, sea-foam green, and dark-chocolate brown, fashioned from microsuede and purchased from the local Sears store.

There is nothing wrong with Sears. I love that place. It's just that I tend to shop there more for tools and toasters than for home fashions for folks who might come to visit at my house. I also think I'm allergic to microsuede. I've never liked the look or feel of it. Yes, punishment to me was making me display a microsuede comforter in my home.

And, truth be told, well, I was going for a little bit different look in that room.

I envisioned some shabby-chic whimsy to go along with the antique bed and repainted desk and dresser from my childhood. Maybe lilac and lemon. Or peach and periwinkle. Light. Airy. Girly. Fresh.

Instead, on a trip to Sears to buy something practical, my dear husband spied this manly looking, hotel bedspreadlike comforter. He thought it would go perfectly in the spare room. I thought it would look nice staying right where it was on the store shelf.

But I obliged. We bought it. It now has a new home.

In an effort to run damage control, I did my best to locate

decor that would blend in with the color scheme. We painted the walls a soothing celery green and the desk and dresser a milky, cream white. I bought some cute pewter drawer pulls and knobs. I found a clearance wreath. And some wall art. And a charming retro windup alarm clock. And you know what?

That guest room isn't half bad. I actually kind of like it (okay—minus the spread!). It reminds me that things can still be beautiful even if I don't get to dictate every detail.

Only God . . .

Learning to let go has been a long, hard process. I am nowhere near living a relinquished life 100 percent of the time. Not even close.

But I am more agreeable, more moldable, less willing to fight, and more willing to acquiesce.

I actually like living a life that is out of control. And do you want to know why?

Not only because, on a dare from a friend, I tried it, actually lived to tell about it, and discovered that it made my life better and my relationships with my family, friends, and even God deeper. But I also like letting go because of two powerful lessons I have learned through the pruning process.

First, trying to be in control isn't a godly goal. In fact, it's quite the opposite.

When we women try to be so on top of things—around the house, at work, in our marriages, in our parenting, and in community ventures—we think we're only taking our jobs seriously, performing our tasks with care, and carrying out the duties of our roles in a way that is excellent and thorough. So give us a break. We really are just trying to please God, right?

I thought so. Sometimes I still think so. However, I happened upon a thought just a year or two ago that makes me wonder this: In attempting to be in command and control, are we trying to be godly or are we trying to be *God*?

Ouch.

Think about it.

Only God can be everywhere.

Only God can know everything.

Only God can see all.

Only God is all-powerful.

Only God can fix the situation or right the wrong or know the future.

Only God can do it all, so why do we mere mortal women even try?

Trying to do it all is trying to be like God. Do you know what happened to a being who once tried to be like God? Read this:

> How you are fallen from heaven,
>   O Day Star, son of Dawn!
> How you are cut down to the ground,
>   you who laid the nations low!
> You said in your heart,
>   "I will ascend to heaven;
> above the stars of God
>   I will set my throne on high;
> I will sit on the mount of assembly
>   in the far reaches of the north;
> I will ascend above the heights of the clouds;
>   *I will make myself like the Most High.*"
> But you are brought down to Sheol
>   to the far reaches of the pit.
>
> (Isaiah 14:12–15 ESV, emphasis added)

That passage from the Old Testament is talking about Satan. Once an angel of light, he got the silly (and stupid) notion is his head one day that he would try to be like God. It was a foolish goal. Not only was it impossible, but the selfish plan got him on the receiving end of the Lord's boot, banished from the Celestial City, kicked out of paradise. Why?

Pride.

Reread the passage. Notice all the "I wills"?

Sometimes proclaiming, "I will" will get us nothing but a very hard landing and in a high heap of trouble. When we launch off uttering our own string of "I wills," we're displaying pride. And in reality, we're trying to be like the Most High.

Trying to do it all isn't a godly pursuit; it's a microemulation of the Enemy. Let's not do that anymore, okay?

In Light of Eternity

The second lesson I've learned in letting go is to embrace the relinquished life, because I've had quite a few opportunities to discover just what matters most in life. And guess what? What matters isn't that I get my own way. What matters is people. Human beings, plain and simple. And the most important being of all is God. When I learn to run my decisions (or indecisions) and my resulting actions through a new grid, I get new behavior. This is my grid:

In light of eternity, is this really important?

I've been warned once or twice by some "I've been there" friends who are also writers not to pen a book about a topic on which I'm not willing to be challenged, put through the ringer, or tested and tempted on every possible front. I need to be ready to go through the fire to see if I'm merely tapping out words or truly living my message. This book has been no exception. (I think next time I'll write about how hard it is to be a millionaire!)

From the day I received the word that I'd gotten a contract on writing a book about how to stop being a control freak and start trusting God, oodles of situations have arisen where I wanted to be in control but simply couldn't be.

As I sit here typing, my sister-in-love Thais is in a hospital an hour and a half from me. A nine-year breast-cancer survivor, she is once more facing down the deadly disease that came back with a vengeance as aggressive bone cancer, stage four.

Thais is not only my kids' aunt; she is like their second mother, a single gal who stepped in when Todd and I needed to get away. With Aunt Thais's fun-loving personality, we learned not to tell our children to mind themselves for her, but instead, we'd beg them to make sure *she* behaved! (She's pulled all sorts of shenanigans involving runaway minibikes and fireworks and jumbo assault squirt rifles. No wonder our kids always wanted her to babysit!)

Watching my relative and close friend battle to walk with a walker, break bones repeatedly, and be confined to a hospital bed has been difficult for me. I want to fix it. I want to know what to tell her when she asks what she should do when weighing the treatment options. I want to know how much longer she has. Should I race over there right now, making the three-hour round trip, or can I go next week? Will she even still be here next week?

Watching this brave woman adjust to her new normal has also inspired me and given me perspective on what matters in this life. Just after she got this latest diagnosis, she talked to me about material things, saying they really didn't matter to her anymore. Having already lived through one bout with cancer, she has learned to live life not so driven, to slow down and savor the moments with friends, or to just sit, open Bible in her lap, and soak in the presence of the Lord.

Most of all, her simple, childlike gratitude has inspired me. A few months ago, after breaking her femur bone by just getting out of bed, she had to have a metal rod inserted in her thigh. I stayed with her all through the surgery and slept in a chair by her bedside all night.

Early the next morning when she opened her eyes, the sunrise was reflecting off the mirrored windows of the towering children's hospital across the street. She glanced at the bright and glorious image. Then she spotted a bouquet of wildflowers from her own backyard that her neighbor had brought up the night before. Without hesitation, after laying eyes on both of these, she looked out the window and up to the sky and declared, "Oh, God, why are you always so good to me?"

This from a woman whose life's story line reads like a bad country song. Two-time cancer patient. A woman whose unwanted divorce took both her large, gorgeous home and her financial security. Then a brain injury that left her unable to work to boot.

How many of us would instead be angry? Would want to know why? Would be bitter and jealous of those with easier roads to take? Would demand, "Get me out of here!" instead of looking for the reasons he brought us here?

Her first utterance upon awakening from a serious surgery due to a terminal illness was to burst with immense gratitude. (And her second declaration was her insistence that she and I had ridden on a bus to California that night with Tom Cruise, who had asked her to be his date to the prom. Pesky drugs!)

I watch my sister-in-love closely. She is grateful. And humble. She accepts the bad, and somehow, wallowing in the middle of the muck, she still sees the tiny flower and gets giddy and grateful. She doesn't try to alter her circumstances. She accepts

211

them, embracing all God is teaching her as she obediently takes the next step toward the unknown on earth but the certain in heaven. She forms her words and makes her choices not in light of "what's in it for me?" but in light of eternity.

When I grow up, I want to be just like her.

A Lesson from South of the Border

I sometimes think we modern women living in our Western, affluent culture have it much too easy. We have too many choices. We have too many opportunities to have ourselves a pity party when we aren't pampered and coddled. It threatens to make us big ole whining, high-maintenance brats.

The native women I met on a missions trip to Mexico in college weren't at all this way. They had very limited wardrobes from which to select. No fancy pots and pans. No stunning decor or state-of-the-art cars. They really had very few decisions to make each day.

Breakfast was always eggs and refried beans. Lunch was beans and rice. Dinner again brought beans and rice and maybe a little meat too. Sometimes there was fruit. And always tortillas, three times a day, made fresh and delicious. They worked hard caring for their children and cleaning the house, sweeping the same dirt floors day after day. They worked in their gardens and went to church gatherings several times a week. Their existence was one of the most monotonous and unglamorous I've ever known. And you know something else?

They were also some of the most content and purposeful women I have ever known. They loved God and their families, and they worked hard just to live daily life. They didn't seem to have any real sense of drive or direction, but they had purpose.

These women weren't overly controlling or desirous of getting their own way. And they possessed the pure joy many of us never experience. Their singing was exuberant, their smiles downright contagious.

Alter and Altar

So how can we acquire the attitude and actions these women displayed? Is it even possible as we dwell in our decision-over-loaded, too-many-privileges, "it's all about me" culture?

Yes, it is.

But we must alter.

And altar.

We must alter our mind-sets; willingly decide to let go. To purpose in our minds and hearts that we don't have to always get our way and that by not getting it, we gain even more. More faith. More peace. More harmony and love.

We must alter our actions. Could we step back and let others lead? Could we defer and then follow, keeping our mouths shut as we do?

We must alter our desired outcomes. No longer should our cravings be control and command. We should instead pine for position — the position God wants us squarely in. Yes, sometimes we lead. Other times we follow. Sometimes we step up. Other times we stand side by side. Always with kindness and grace. Yes, we must know — and accept — our place.

And we must alter our speech, erase the harsh words hurled in haste, the cutting comments spoken seemingly in jest (but really meant to wound). Our words should be loving, direct if they must be, truthful, and without malice. Remember, our words only spill out what's already inside.

Yes, we must alter.

We must come to the altar.

At the altar we lay down our rights, our wrongs, our desire for control, our need to constantly have the upper hand. It can be a crucial sacrifice of an issue that is immense. Or it may be simply holding our tongues when it comes time to pick the fast-food eatery and going with the choice of our spouses or friends, being thankful just to have food to eat and a warm building in which to enjoy it.

The altar is where we offer ourselves to God and his service. Where we commit our lives to his plan. It's where we pray that he will bring our thoughts and our resulting actions in line with his Word and his will. Where we know our place. And where we give him his proper place too.

God is God and we are not.

He is the Potter. We are waiting lumps of unformed clay. If we allow him to have his way, he can make something stunning in both function and form. If we allow him to mold us, we will be fit for service and kingdom work. If instead we stiffen and insist on running the show our own way, we may end up lop-sided, good-for-little vessels that settle instead of soar.

Yes, it's true: the out-of-control life is a refreshingly thrilling ride. When we relinquish control, let go and "let God," we find our faith and the cadence of life that notices the small things and the beauty in all.

Will you try it?

Will you trust God?

Will you stop running the show and start walking in faith?

Will you loosen your grip on life and grab tightly to the edge of his garment? He will see and respond. He indeed can heal us all of our misplaced grasping for things that aren't ours to decide, or ours to do or to have. If we but lean hard into his loving arms and find our safe and secure place, we can discover the thrill of being both completely out of control and smack-dab in the center of his will — the adventure of the relinquished life.

Trust me, there's no more thrilling ride. And the impact on your relationships will bring calm to your spirit and contentment to your heart.

Are you with me?

I double dare you to do it.

For I know, dear sister, in his strength you can.

Are you ready?

On your mark . . .

Get set . . .

LET. IT. GO!

Acknowledgments

To my Proverbs 31 Ministries sisters under the leadership of President Lysa TerKeurst, Executive Director of Radio and Devotions Renee Swope, and Executive Director of Operations LeAnn "The Queen" Rice: To think I am part of this team! I pinch myself daily. A special shout out to Glynnis Whitwer, Amy Carroll, Samantha Reed, Melissa Taylor, Barb Spencer, Teri Bucholtz, Sheila Magnum, Angie Combs, Lisa Boyd, and the rest of our band of ordinary women who together get to serve our extraordinary God. Let's chant it together, girls, "Graceful, godly, and ready to go!"

To my agent Esther Fedorkevich: For your straight-shooting, Jersey-accented advice and encouragement. You made this Midwestern mom believe in God's call on her life when she wanted to throw in the towel and go eat her weight in dark chocolate. Oh, yeah . . . and for being a Mets fan — you are forgiven. Go Tigers!

To Lori Vandenbosch: Oh, dangling participles! This book wouldn't exist without your writing expertise. For your keen content insight, stellar grammar skills, and many gentle scratch-it-and-start-all-overs, I am forever grateful. Okay. Sometimes those actually kinda ticked me off, but you knew what you were doing!!!!!! (Excessive exclamation points inserted just for you, my dear.)

To my new Zondervan family: Tonya Osterhouse for your editing prowess; Londa Alderink for your tireless marketing efforts; Robin Phillips for being my biggest cheerleader and for your patience with this curriculum newbie; Sandy VanderZicht for continually believing in me and wearing way-cool scarves; Carolyn McCready and Cindy Lambert—friendly faces from my past who invest in my future; and also Don Gates, Tracy Danz, Chris Fann, John Raymond, and TJ Rathbun. Your work both pleases God and blesses me.

To Jeanette Thomason, my very first editor and sweet, now-lifelong friend: For your willingness to take a chance on an unknown Michigan stay-at-home mom with ideas in her head and an old hand-me-down laptop in her hands, I sincerely thank you. Again. And again. And forever.

To my Cyber Sisters, who pray, give feedback, and then pray some more: Thanks for letting me toss titles, concepts, covers, and other random things your way to solicit your honest feedback. I love praying for you too. You rocketh!

To the three wonderful churches I have been a part of over the past twenty-six years of my adult life: Pilgrim Methodist, St. Johns First Baptist, and Northpointe Community. (Yep! I'm a spiritual mutt.) It has been an honor to serve alongside you as we seek to glorify God. Can't wait 'til we all get to heaven and can worship him together . . . FOREVER!

To my personal prayer team of Kelly Hovermale, Marcia Stump, Debi Davis, Suzy Williams, Dorothy Prins, Heather Vanderlaan, Becky Glenn, Patricia Esch, Amber Fuller, Tammy Underwood, Joyce Ashley, and Cindy Bultema: Your support enables me to both live life and serve God. I don't ever take for granted the time you spend petitioning God for me, my family, and the women I serve. Thank you.

To Steve and Claire Bancroft and family: For your willingness to open your home and your hearts in a totally unselfish way. Your family is amazing. Crazy, too, but still amazing.

To other random ministry chicklets: Hearts at Home's Jill Savage, Brenda Paccamonti, Lisa Reilly, Megan Kaeb, and Rhonda Kasper; online magazine RooMag.com's fearless-and-fabulous leader Candace Cameron Bure, along with editors Ruth Schwenk and Clare Smith; fellow bloggers/writers Courtney Joseph, Darlene Schacht, Julie Barnhill*, Nicole O'Dell, and Rachel Wojnarowski. Your love for God and desire to help women continually inspires me.

To my fab four "Spiritual Shield" of Mary Steinke, Lindsey Feldpausch, Sharon Glasgow, and my executive assistant, Kim Cordes: You hem me in — going before me, behind me, to my left, and to my right. For each day pounding heaven on my behalf and fighting against Satan's constant schemes . . . oh . . . *I can hardly find the words!* If it weren't for you, I'd chuck it all, grab a Cheerwine soda, and flop on the couch to watch old black-and-white movies all day. But because of you, I see God move despite my countless imperfections and crippling insecurities. And so, I keep going. And he keeps working. All because *you* keep doing battle.

To my extended family on both the Patterson/Sanders and Ehman/Motyer sides. What can I say? We look like a stinkin' sitcom. But we are family and I love us!

To daughter, Kenna — my close friend and the most fly-by-the-seat-of-her-pants-but-always-land-standing-up gal I know: You love Jesus and people. Despite our novice parenting skills, you turned out to be an amazing woman. And I still have no clue where the fashion and cosmetology skills come from, but I'm grateful for the lifetime of free services! (Can you fly home this weekend? My roots need touching up.)

To sons Mitchell and Spencer: Your polar-opposite personalities make for great entertainment. Still you get along famously 92 percent of the time. (The other 8 percent? Knock off the fighting already before somebody breaks a lamp!) I love watching you play sports and devour my cooking. And now that this project is finished, I promise there will be more meals of the homemade kind and less ... well ... you know ... frozen pizzas. ☺ (Sam's Club's profits are plunging as I type.) Remember God has a plan for your life. Follow it, not the world.

To my college sweetheart and handsome hubster, Todd: I. STILL. DO. You are the strong, steady string that tethers this runaway kite of a girl. I really wish God would change that whole "no marriage in heaven" thing. I'd stay hitched to you for eternity. ☺

And to my sweet Jesus: For dying for me and then teaching me daily to die to myself.

I adore and am grateful to you all!

*NOTE: Actually doesn't do anything inspiring but would expect her name to be listed. ☺ Just kidding, Jules! Grab a box of Ho Hos® and a six-pack of Pepsi and meet me at the lake. We've got politics, theology, and trivial matters to discuss.

Notes

1. To learn more about Unveiling Glory, visit their website at http://www.unveilinglory.com.

2. Dr. Julianna Slattery, *Finding the Hero in Your Husband: Surrendering the Way God Intended* (Deerfield Beach, Fla.: Faith Communications, 2001), 121.

3. Amy Carmichael, quoted in Amber Penney, "What's Love Look Like?," Christian Classics, *Campus Life* (2001), accessed March 31, 2012, http://www.christianitytoday.com/iyf/faithandlife/christianclassics/20.50.html.

Karen Ehman is a *New York Times* bestselling author, a Proverbs 31 Ministries speaker, and a writer for *Encouragement For Today*, an online devotional that reaches over 4 million users daily. She has written 14 books and Bible studies including *Keep It Shut: What to Say, How to Say It and When to Say Nothing at All* and *Keep Showing Up: How to Stay Crazy in Love When Your Love Drives You Crazy*. Her passion is to help women to live their priorities as they reflect the gospel to a watching world.

Karen has been featured on numerous media outlets including TODAY Show Parents, FoxNews.com, Redbook.com, Crosswalk .com, *FamilyLife*, Focus on the Family, and *HomeLife* Magazine. Married to her college sweetheart, Todd, and the mother of three (plus one daughter-in-love), she enjoys collecting and using vintage kitchenware, cheering for the Detroit Tigers, and feeding the many people who gather around her kitchen island for a taste of Mama Karen's cooking.

Connect with her at karenehman.com or on Instagram (@ karenehman), Twitter (@karen_ehman) Pinterest (karenehmanp31) or Facebook (OfficialKarenEhman).

Proverbs 31
MINISTRIES

ABOUT PROVERBS 31 MINISTRIES

If you were inspired by Karen Ehman and desire to deepen your own personal relationship with Jesus Christ, I encourage you to connect with Proverbs 31 Ministries.

Proverbs 31 Ministries exists to be a trusted friend who will take you by the hand and walk by your side, leading you one step closer to the heart of God through:

- Free online daily devotions
- First 5 Bible study app
- Online Bible studies
- Podcast
- Daily radio program
- Books and resources

For more information about Proverbs 31 Ministries, visit www.Proverbs31.org.

New Video Study for Your Church or Small Group

If you've enjoyed this book, now you can go deeper with the companion video Bible study!

In this six-session study, Karen Ehman helps you apply the principles in *Let. It. Go.* to your life. The study guide includes video notes, group discussion questions, and personal study and reflection materials for in-between sessions.

Study Guide
9780310684541

DVD
9780310684534

Available now at your favorite bookstore, or streaming video on StudyGateway.com.

Keep Showing Up

How to Stay Crazy in Love When Your Love Drives You Crazy

Karen Ehman, New York Times bestselling author

It is true that opposites attract–for a while. But often as the years go by in our marriages, opposites may also begin to attack. The habits and characteristics we once found endearing about our significant other are the exact things that drive us crazy years later!

Whether you and your spouse disagree about finances, parenting, or how to load the dishwasher, your differences don't need to divide you. They can actually bring you closer together--and closer to God.

In *Keep Showing Up*, Karen Ehman will help you to...

- Play to each other's strengths as you work on your own weaknesses
- Become a faithful forgiver who also forgets
- Discover strategies for avoiding the social media comparison trap
- Resist the dangerous tendency to mimic a friend's marriage
- Unearth the magic in the midst of the mundane
- Experience how a spouse who drives you crazy can drive you straight to Jesus

Throughout *Keep Showing Up*, Karen includes ideas to strengthen your marriage right now, such as how to find your calling as a couple, date-night discussion starters, and tips for rediscovering romance in the midst of the routine. Learn how your "incompatibility" can actually become the strength of your marital team in this real-life guide to both living with and loving your spouse—differences and all.

Available in stores and online!